modus cooperandi
performance through collaboration

Modus Cooperandi Press
A Division of Modus Cooperandi, Inc.
1818 Westlake Avenue North, Suite 308
Seattle, WA 98109

Designed by Jim Benson
Manufactured in the United States of America

ISBN 978-0-578-00214-9

Scrumban

And Other Essays on Kanban Systems for Lean
Software Development

By Corey Ladas

TABLE OF CONTENTS

ACKNOWLEDGEMENTS

First, I thank Jim Benson and David Anderson for making it possible to write this book at all. David has given me many ideas over the years and gave me a truly uncommon opportunity to study and apply many of the ideas that are documented in this book. Jim Benson convinced me to scale back my ambitions and publish something smaller and more focused. Jim has contributed a good deal of effort toward transforming a pile of text into a book.

Mary Poppendieck, J.D. Meier, and John Hunter each recognized my writing early on and helped me to find my focus and reach a receptive audience. A new publication can easily run out of steam once the initial novelty of the subject matter wears off. Such high-caliber encouragement can provide a lot of motivation to continue beyond the rush of the opening bell.

Bernie Thompson hosts the Lean Software Engineering website and contributes wise and thoughtful commentary less often than I would like him to. He has also been a good friend and colleague through good times and bad.

Karl Scotland and Eric Willeke are fellow pioneers in the application of Lean Thinking to software development and have provided ongoing inspiration, support, and stimulating discussion. They each contributed detailed and thoughtful reviews of this book and caught a number of things that otherwise might have been quite embarrassing.

Finally, I want to thank Eric Brechner for believing in me and inspiring me to write about something that I felt strongly about. The quarrelsome voice and sly dialectical reasoning behind Eric's I.M. Wright persona are in no small way an inspiration behind my own narrative style. But most of all, Eric was a good friend to me at a time when I needed it most.

INTRODUCTION

This book is about an emerging body of knowledge that is currently brewing within the Agile software development community. The object of this body of knowledge is Agile Workflow Management. The theories applied to this problem are Lean Thinking and the Theory of Constraints. The specific practices applied are kanban systems, drum-buffer-rope systems, and throughput metrics.

Early thinking in Agile software development seemed very focused around detailed activities of code creation and deployment, and around small, self-contained, technically-heavy teams. Agile methods have gained popularity over the years, and the scope of some of these methods, particularly Scrum, has expanded to cover an ever-larger part of software project management. As many project managers and project management practices have been displaced by this growth, some existing capability and areas of expertise seem to have been tossed out with the bathwater. There has been a trend over the last couple of years to patch some remedial capability into the skill set of a new generation of Agile managers, including more serious thinking about product design, risk management, and financial accountability. Workflow management is one of those core competencies that I hope to see reintegrated into contemporary thinking on software development. Because like it or not, a large proportion of software development problems have very natural workflows that deserve to be managed well.

When descriptions of Scrum first began to appear in the industry literature many years ago, my imagination was captured most by the metaphors that were used to describe it. I thought that the whole "Sprints & Scrum Masters" model was a cute example, probably useful for some simple problems, mostly useful as a simple explanation for novices. What I really found valuable was the analogy itself:

> *Software development processes can be*
> *described in terms of queues and control loops,*
> *and managed accordingly.*

It did not take me too long to connect this interpretation with a similar conclusion reached by Donald Reinertsen in *Managing the Design Factory*. From there it was a short hop to the rest of the Lean world. If Scrum could work, then Lean could work, and Lean was obviously a much more powerful theory. Once the Poppendiecks' *Lean Software Development* admitted that possibility, the gauntlet was thrown, the cat was let out of the bag, and it was only a matter of time before Agile would be subject to a major overhaul with respect to Lean principles. David Anderson's *Agile Management* put newly minted Agile teams on notice that they would eventually be treated like the businesses that they are and held accountable for their results. Denne and Cleland-Huang's *Software by Numbers* described in some detail how that could be done.

I think that a large part of the Scrum community has made an error in over-committing to a specific process that is narrow, prescriptive, and rigid--what Jeff Sutherland came to christen "Type A Scrum." More like me, Jeff's way of thinking about the subject seems to be more grammatical and compositional. If more people followed Jeff's interpretation of Scrum, we might be in a better position than we are today, and ideas like the ones discussed in this book might seem more obvious and less heretical. It's a much smaller step from Type C Scrum to a Kanban pull system than it is from Type A Scrum.

Which is not to say that Type A Scrum is "wrong." Scrum is very effective for certain types of problems. Scrum works best for a backlog of mixed work item types with no consistent workflow. It can also be effective for a backlog of work items of a similar type, but with a poorly defined workflow. But just to be clear, Extreme Programming is a very well defined workflow, so if you can apply XP to your project, you're already an excellent candidate for Kanban. Scrum can also be useful as a starting point for an experienced Agile team to evolve into a Leaner process. I have always assumed that I am writing for that audience, and such an evolution is the "Scrumban" process that gives this book its title.

I also think that the Product Owner role is an especially egregious error that trivializes the problems of product planning, product design, and requirements analysis and hides them behind a black-box role that encompasses at least much complexity as the "development" part of the software creation process. The right answer to the wrong question is still the wrong answer i.e. software development is garbage-in-garbage-out It's hard not to smell a little bit of class rivalry in the rhetoric of Scrum true believers, keeping the suits out of the hair of the geeks. One of the goals of a Lean software development process should be the end-to-end integration of the value stream, from user research and strategic planning to data center operations and product support. Or as the Poppendiecks say, "from concept to cash." I address that problem by admitting a much larger definition of "team" than the very programmer-centered model of early Agile thought.

Time and popularity have exposed some of the limitations of Scrum as experienced in the real world. Some of that clearly falls under the "you're doing it wrong" category, but some is also perfectly legitimate criticism of real weaknesses in the method. I adopted Scrum fairly early, and observed its operation in a high-stress, edge-case environment that clearly exposed some of its limitations. Over time, the chorus of the dissatisfied has grown to the point of being its own recognizable community with a set of consistent observations and opinions. This is the way it should be. For some of us, what seemed "good enough" many years ago no longer seems good enough today.

For me, one of the most important facts about Lean is that it is defined as a set of principles, and not as a process that can be replicated across environments. The Toyota Production System is Lean, but Lean is not the Toyota Production System. We are not trying to make software development look more like manufacturing, because Lean is not about manufacturing. Lean is about value streams. Lean is the 5 principles that were given by James Womack and Daniel Jones, because that is how they have defined it. Those 5 principles can manifest themselves in a variety of expressions, one of which is the Toyota Production System. Today, a growing number of practitioners are applying those 5 principles to software development. We have learned something about what is possible, and we feel confident in calling our results Lean, even though we know that we are only beginning and that there is great deal more to learn.

Since I have a recent historical example of what not to do in the promotion of a new method, I have sworn to treat the promotion of software development kanban systems differently. Kanban is not a process. Kanban is a practice that embodies a principle. Kanban is a mechanism that can be used to compose a process which will always be specific to the problem at hand and the resources available. If anybody ever tells you that the "right" way to do kanban is to replicate something that some itinerant guru has done, then they are mistaken. Those stories are examples and only examples. Your process will be different. Self-organization and continuous improvement demand that this be so.

TWO AXIOMS OF LEAN SOFTWARE DEVELOPMENT

There are a variety of principles to choose from when considering adoption of lean software development, such as the "2 pillars of the Toyota Production System," or the "14 principles of the Toyota Way," or "5 principles of Lean Thinking," or "7 principles of Lean Software Development," or even "Deming's 14 principles of management." And of course, there's always the old "Agile Manifesto."

While I think there's value in most of those things, so much choice leaves a lot of room for interpretation. That can be a good thing, but it leaves me searching for something more fundamental. Before I can get into questions like "why should I be lean?" or "what should I believe in order to be lean?," first, I have to ask a deeper question: *under what conditions is lean software development possible?*

You might need some of those other principles in order to act on your goal, but you may not get very far until you are clear about the most basic premises of the problem. To that end, I propose two simple axioms:

Axiom 1: *It is possible to divide the work into small value-adding increments that can be independently scheduled.*

The first axiom is not specific to lean software development. It is the premise behind iterative, evolutionary, and Agile development, and has been studied and applied for many decades. It might continue to be a difficult concept for some, but not due to any lack of literature or examples in the world. If iterative development is possible, then lean development may also be possible.

Axiom 2: *It is possible to develop any value-adding increment in a continuous flow from requirement to deployment.*

The second axiom is more specific to lean development. Lean's evolutionary predecessors have had much to say about problem definition, team composition, and development practices, but less to say about workflow and detailed operational scheduling. Agile, in particular, seems to encourage a romantic trade-guild culture that resists the kind of systematic discipline that is required for lean thinking. Continuous flow implies we're going to have to say a lot about how people can work together in order to avoid wastes like inventory, delay, rework, and overproduction.

Stating our premises in such stark terms enables us to visualize the problem more clearly:

- What would a continuous flow of new feature development look like?

- What would need to happen, and in what order?

- What resources would need to be available to make that possible?

- How would roles and responsibilities need to be defined in order to make those resources available when needed?

- What is the ideal flow?

- What is the best flow we can achieve with the capability at hand?

- How can we improve in the direction of the ideal?

Then you may find that some of those other principles are necessary to help you realize your goal.

WHY PULL? WHY KANBAN?

People with different skills have to work together to deliver product features. Don't build features that nobody needs right now. Don't write more specs than you can code. Don't write more code than you can test. Don't test more code than you can deploy.

Pretty simple to describe in theory. Some subtlety in practice. A kanban is a tool, and like any tool, it is meant to solve a problem. I think kanban solves this problem more efficiently than the known alternatives.

COFFEE CUP KANBAN

Coffee bars employ a couple of different strategies for taking and filling orders. Each strategy makes different tradeoffs.

Sometimes someone will take your order, ring you up, and then make your drink and give it to you. Other times someone will take your order, mark up a cup with the details of your order, place the cup in a queue to be picked up by a barista who will make the drink and then place it on a shelf and call it out.

That second arrangement is a kanban system, and the cup is the kanban. The cup-ban doubles as an order form that can encode most combinations that a barista should expect.

There are reasons to choose one process over another. Small or lower-volume shops with only one employee on shift usually apply the first method. Larger, higher-volume stores with two or more workers on shift usually apply the second method. The store using the kanban method gains the advantage of taking your order (and collecting your money) quickly. Unfortunately for you, that often means exiting one queue so you can line up in another, more captive queue.

It is good news for you when the barista asks you, "can I get a drink started for you?" because that should mean he has slack capacity. By the time the cashier finishes collecting your money, the drink should already be under construction. The barista shouldn't ask you for a drink order if he already has a queue of cups to process. On the contrary, once the kanban queue starts backing up, the cashier should start stalling, even if that appears to make the cashier queue back up. The second queue has limited capacity before waiting customers start crowding each other or irritating seated customers.

Some shops get obnoxiously long lines during the
morning rush. The solution to that often appears to be
adding an additional espresso machine, because the
making of the drink ends up being the bottleneck.

The trade-off for businesses is that the rushes don't last,
and then the surplus capacity goes unutilized for most of
the day. Still, I know for certain that some shops lose
sales, and even customers because of the lines, so I
don't think that the capacity strategy is employed as
often as it should be.

Watch your coffee cup once your order is taken. It
should never stop flowing. If it does, you should ask
yourself why and imagine what you might do differently.

A KANBAN IS MORE THAN AN INDEX CARD

In a modern economy, the production and distribution of
scarce goods and services are regulated by a system of
money and prices. Money can be represented by
currency notes, which have little intrinsic value, but that

by agreement, can be exchanged for real goods and services. The existence of a neutral medium of exchange makes possible a system of economic calculation of the relative scarcity of the supply of goods in an economy. Such a system of prices is a market. Markets communicate the value of economic production and distribution to their participants.

If a currency note can be exchanged for an object of real value, then there must be some way to enforce the scarcity of the notes in a way that corresponds to the scarcity of real value in the economy. In practice, some kind of institution must enforce this scarcity. The health of a market economy depends greatly on the ability of its monetary institution to coordinate the supply of money with the supply of goods and services. In an unhealthy economy, unstable prices make economic calculation difficult and disrupt the communication between producers and consumers needed for efficient production and distribution.

A kanban represents a portion of the productive capacity of some closed internal economy. It is a medium of exchange for the goods and services provided by the operations of a system of productive resources. The supply of kanban in circulation is controlled by some regulatory function that enforces its value. That is, a kanban is a kind of private currency and the shop floor manager is the bank that issues it, for the purpose of economic calculation.

If you carry the currency analogy further, then you might say that kanban is not about the cards at all. Just like money is not about the bills. Kanban is all about the limits, the quantity in circulation. How that is represented in a transaction is mostly incidental.

A simple rule for understanding all of this might be:

> A task card without a limit is not a kanban in the same way that a photocopy of a dollar bill is not money.

If you use a durable token like a plastic card, then this is easy to manage: control the number of cards in circulation. If all of the available cards are already in circulation, then the next person who comes looking for one is just going to have to wait until one returns. This is the very purpose of the kanban system. However, if you use a more disposable medium like index cards or sticky notes, then you need another mechanism to regulate the "money supply." In our case, we simply write the quantity of kanban in circulation on the task board, and allocate new cards according to that limit.

This means that a kanban serves two functions: it is a request to do something in particular, but it is also permission to do something in general. That second notion of permission is where people who are new to lean thinking tend to struggle. But this is precisely how we can "optimize the whole" or "subordinate to the constraint."

KANBAN SYSTEMS FOR SOFTWARE DEVELOPMENT

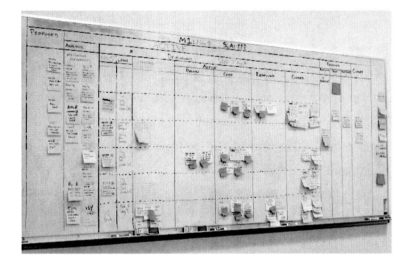

AN IDEAL CASE

Let's imagine an ideal scenario for software development.

In this scenario, there are some users who have real, identifiable needs. Some of these users are paying customers who will gladly give you money if you can deliver value to them. You can express their needs as a set of criteria to be satisfied, and these criteria can be measured. Your customers bring you their business because: not only do you promise to identify what they want and build them a solution, you also promise to deliver a solution quickly.

The flow of information is something like:

latent demand -> characterized demand -> value-adding design -> production -> deployed solution

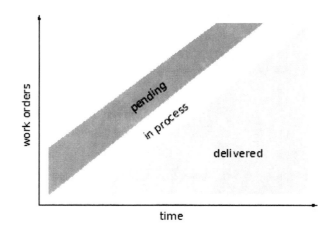

Cumulative Flow Diagram (CFD)

...and your goal is to have smooth and continuous flow through this process, gently accelerating for all eternity. The scope of the demand you can address and the supply you can deliver will continue to grow as long as your own capability continues to grow (*remember that we're talking about an ideal scenario!*).

That is only a very high level description. How might a detailed process to realize such a system look? Imagining in detail how our ideal scenario might work may also give us some ideas for what might be possible in real life (in TRIZ, this practice is called the *Ideal Final Result*).

As information flows through the system, we must have some representation of it:

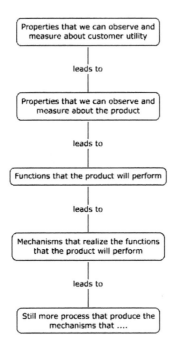

...or...

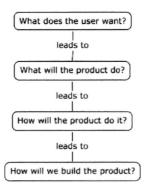

There are many such representations, but let's use:

- *Use case:* a description of how the product will be used, in the context of the user

- *Functional requirement:* an operational definition of what the product will do

- *Design parameter:* an operational definition of how the product will implement a functional requirement

- *Design constraint:* some limitation on what design parameters may be chosen

- *Process variable:* an operational definition of how a design parameter will be produced

Because we always want to deliver new value quickly, we want to limit the amount of work that we take on at one time. The smallest amount means one work request. But one of what? Since we are value-oriented, we will pick *use cases*, since that speaks directly in user terms.

A use case describes the value that the product delivers to the user, roughly by telling a story about how the product will be used. A use case is a structured story, and may make reference to, or be composed of other use cases. A use case will also make reference to functional requirements, as a description of role of the product in the user's story.

A composite use case might be large, so we will decompose new large use cases until they no longer contain or reference other use cases. Such an atomic use case is then a candidate to schedule for development.

A goal for our descriptions of atomic use cases is that they should all be of a similar size. A use case should be testable and traceable to customer satisfaction criteria. A use case should say as much as possible about the user's needs, expectations, and goals, and as little as possible about the design of the product. For convenience, let's call such an atomic use case a *feature*. A feature is the simplest practical expression of: *what does the user want?*

So our system (so far) consists of a process for identifying and describing features, and then scheduling them, one at a time, for further development. The old (and broken) way of development might accumulate a long list of such features, and then give them to somebody to analyze to produce another long list enumerating *what will the product do?* That in turn would be given to somebody else to design, and so on.

But that is *not* what we will do.

As soon as we identify any new feature, we immediately enumerate a short list describing *what will the product do?* Then we will get right to work on a corresponding list describing *how will the product do it?* Then we immediately produce a description of *how will we build the product?* Then we build it.

In other words, we practice depth-first design.

Now, it takes a lot of expertise to design a product of any significance, so a team of experts will somehow have to work together and coordinate with one another to make all of this happen without tripping over one another's feet. *It's one thing to say that we're going to deliver one feature at a time, but how, exactly are WE going to do that?*

And that question is precisely what makes this story interesting.

IN SEARCH OF ONE-PIECE FLOW

There are a few ways to go about this, so let's start with something simple, see where that falls short, and work our way up to a better solution. Let us also assume that there is a common workflow that will be applied to each work request.

CRAFT PRODUCTION

Imagine a small team of generalists. As new work orders appear in the incoming queue, each idle team member will take ownership of one work order until there are no pending work orders or no idle team members. This effectively sets a work-in-process (WIP) limit equal to the size of the team. Each assigned team member applies the workflow to one requirement, continuously, until the requirement is integrated and deployed. A team member may only own one work order at a time. Upon completion, the team member then returns to the idle pool for reassignment.

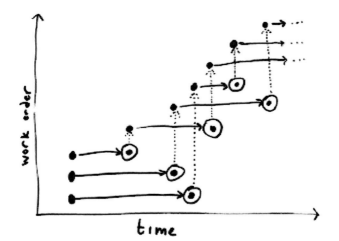

Craft production pros:

- incoming work-in-process is controlled
- defined workflow is possible
- pull is possible
- one piece flow is possible
- variation in the size of work orders is buffered

Craft production cons:

- generalists are slower than specialists
- competent generalists are rare
- knowledge transfer is hindered
- standardized work is hindered
- quality is inconsistent
- accountability is limited
- process improvement feedback is limited

While the craft production style of working controls the flow of work and creates some degree of predictability, this process is basically a series of one-offs conducted by generalists who take a task from inception to completion. This means that some key elements of a specialized work flow are lost. These include informal or formal reviews at hand-offs, lack of knowledge transfer from one team member to another, and a general decrease in quality as focus falls to task completion and not task quality.

There may be some elements of lean thinking in such a process, but it is not a lean process.

FEATURE CREW

If it is not possible to assemble enough generalists to implement effective craft production, then perhaps small multidisciplinary teams could work. A *feature crew* contains a small set of workers with complementary skills necessary to complete the work efficiently.

Work orders are defined in such a way to engage the team for a few days or a few weeks. In this case, the work-in-process limit is made equal to the number of teams available.

As new work orders appear in the incoming queue, each idle feature team will take ownership of one work order until there are no pending work orders or no idle teams. The assigned feature team applies the workflow to the requirement, continuously, until the requirement is integrated and deployed. The feature team may only own one requirement at a time. Upon completion, the feature team then returns to the idle pool to be reassigned or recombined.

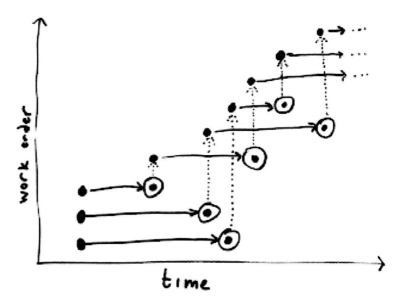

Feature crew pros:

- incoming work-in-process is controlled
- defined workflow is possible
- pull is possible
- one piece flow is possible
- variation in the size of work orders is buffered
- division of labor

Feature crew cons:

- specialists are hoarded
- resources are underutilized
- knowledge diffuses slowly
- standardized work is limited
- quality is inconsistent
- process improvement feedback is limited

Feature crews have most of the advantages of solitary craft production, and fewer disadvantages. Within the feature team, people will self-organize around the workflow. Resource utilization will be lower than the simple craft mode, but productivity loss will be offset by specialization and division of labor. Knowledge transfer will be greater if teams are periodically recombined.

These craft production approaches are essentially the domain of Agile development. While we could continue to explore the possibilities by evaluating various Agile methods, we will still be in the domain of craft production, so let's back up and try a different approach altogether.

SYNCHRONIZED WORKFLOW

The principle, *Schedule is Orthogonal to Workflow*, suggests that there are two fundamental approaches to partitioning work: by schedule or by workflow. Traditional project management schedules large work orders and aligns resources by workflow. Agile/craft methods schedule small work orders and align resources by schedule.

Why doesn't anybody try to schedule small work orders and align resources by workflow? I don't know...so let's try it!

Imagine that you have a small cross functional team. There is one specialist for each step in the workflow, a classic division of labor.

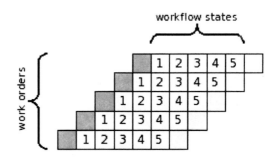

Work in process is limited to the number of steps in the workflow, and hence to the number or team members. The work is synchronized according to a clock. In other words, this is a discrete pipeline.

At the first clock tick, a work order is pulled from a queue and placed in the first processing state. At the second clock tick, the first work order is moved to the second processing state and a new work order is set in process. Once the pipeline is full, each clock tick completes one work order, begins a new work order, and advances work-in-process to the next step.

In order for this to work efficiently, there must be limited variation:

- in the size of work orders,
- between the durations of different processing states to complete any work order, and
- within any specific processing state.

This is a very rigid system. Excellent for, say, lawnmower assembly. However, none of those conditions will be probable in any kind of creative process like software development.

Synchronization will only be possible if you set the clock interval proportional to the worst case duration of any of the processing states. That would give you control at the cost of enormous waste of delay.

Synchronized workflow pros:

- incoming work-in-process is controlled
- standardized work is possible
- pull is possible
- division of labor
- knowledge transfer
- transparency and accountability
- process improvement feedback

Synchronized workflow cons:

- variation in the size of incoming work orders is difficult to control
- process variation will cause delay and/or inventory between workflow steps
- resources will thrash between underutilization and overutilization
- does not accommodate design iteration
- pipeline stalls disrupt flow

The fundamental problem with synchronized workflow is too much variation in product development for work to be strictly synchronized. However, the idea of aligning resources by workflow has much more potential than this simplistic case.

TASK LEVELING

It is natural to want to align a design workflow with the logical boundaries of the activities involved. However, if we are trying to synchronize work, it is unlikely that the logical boundaries of tasks will align well with the clock:

...which means that people will always be waiting for the bottleneck to finish its work:

It should be possible (even desirable) to break large activities into smaller, similarly-sized pieces:

You might even interleave some of the activities in order to smooth out the flow of information from one brain to another:

If the variation in the completion time of each of the tasks is under control, then the pipeline can flow.

A long pipeline of small steps will carry a lot of work-in-process. The cost of a pipeline stall will be lower, but the *probability* of a stall will be higher. Considerable slack may be needed to buffer variation in the cycle time for component tasks. However, related tasks can be combined into task groups:

| analyze and design | design and test | test, build, deploy |

...where the task group is internally self-organized and externally synchronized:

		analyze and design	design and test	test, build, deploy
	analyze and design	design and test	test, build, deploy	
analyze and design	design and test	test, build, deploy		

By recombining things in such a way, we can also apply pooled-variance-style buffering to each task group, in order to reduce the total amount or buffering required to keep things moving.

CONCURRENT PIPELINES

If all work moves through a single pipeline, then a stall
in that pipeline will disrupt everything. The penalty for a
pipeline stall is reduced with more than one pipeline.
Additionally, a single pipeline can only carry one
pipeline's worth of capacity. We can expand capacity
and smooth out disruptions at the same time by adding
a second pipeline:

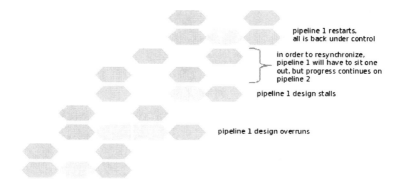

pipeline 1 restarts,
all is back under control

in order to resynchronize,
pipeline 1 will have to sit one
out, but progress continues on
pipeline 2

pipeline 1 design stalls

pipeline 1 design overruns

The capacity of a single unstalled pipeline will be 100%
minus whatever buffering is needed to optimize stalls vs
slack time. Maybe full capacity is 80%. If a lone pipeline
stalls, capacity is 0%. If one of two stalls, capacity is
still 40%. 1:3 is 53% and so on. If there is a 25%
chance of a stall in any clock tick, then there's a 6%
chance of 2:2 stalling, and so on.

Management overhead will scale linearly for a while. Will
management overhead eventually scale to a point where
a different organization is more efficient? Most likely.

We're getting pretty creative with our efforts to make this pipeline idea work! I don't know if we'll ever be able to control work order variation enough to make this viable, but we've certainly identified some ideas that are worth exploring further. Now, we'll relax the requirement for synchronization and look at more ideas about using buffers to smooth out the variation between tasks and work orders.

KANBAN SYNCHRONIZATION

The pipeline model shares a common problem with network model scheduling. Variation in product development activities is simply too hard to control. Pipelines and network models can be made to work by adding a lot of time padding, and indeed, we started to resort to Critical Chain-style buffer management methods to try to make the pipeline work.

We can do something to manage the variation in work orders by controlling coupling and by specifying requirements according to a well defined schema that limits complexity. Those things help, but they are more order-of-magnitude levels of control.

Even if we could control work order size to, say, a factor of two, we'd still have the problem of variation within the workflow. Some requirements may be easy to design, but devilishly difficult to test, perhaps for instrumental reasons. There might be a simple and elegant design that almost matches the requirement and a monstrously complex design that exactly matches it. How long something takes might depend on who gets the assignment. High value problems are uncertain. Uncertainty is risk. Sometimes risk doesn't go your way.

So a viable solution will have to do its best to control variation while still operating within the reality-based paradigm. Given the challenge, it is unsurprising that craft production is attractive to practitioners, but we can do better.

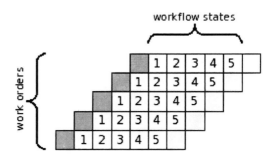

If you take a horizontal slice across the cumulative flow diagram of a development process, you get the sequence of the workflow for a particular work order. If you take a vertical slice, you get a snapshot of all of the current work-in-process. Curiously, with our pipeline model, these two sequences are the same:

analyze analyze design design design test test build deploy

Not only are they the same, they're always the same. A consequence of our pipeline design is that it strictly limits work-in-process according to the proportions of the workflow. That's good! That is what we want.

Is there a way to more directly control work-in-process that allows for more variation than clock synchronization?

WIP AND FLOW

Imagine that we make a pooled workcell, in which each station represents one step in the logical workflow of our hypothetical feature design process.

analyze 2	design 3	test 2	build 1	deploy 1

Each station has a work-in-process limit that corresponds to the time proportion of that state in the workflow. The limit governs the maximum number of work items that can be in that state at any instant. In

this case, the *analyze* and *test* states have limits of 2.
The *design* state has a limit of 3, and *build* and *deploy*
have limits of 1.

If a state is below its limit, then it may take possession
of a work item from a preceding state upon that work
item's completion by the preceding state. If a state is at
its limit, it must wait for one of its own items to
complete and be pulled into a downstream state before
it can pull an item from an upstream state.

Without any further intervention, this design is already
far less susceptible to stalls than any of our
synchronized designs. If 2 out of 3 work items in a
workflow state exceed the control limit on completion
time, the rest of the system will continue to function.
Even if an entire state locks up, it will take time for the
upstream states to back up and the downstream states
to starve. In the meantime, management will have
ample warning to intervene. Flow will resume naturally
once capacity is added or the obstacle is cleared.

BUFFERS IN SPACE VERSUS TIME

Most future events in a project plan will occur according to the sort of long-tailed probability distribution that you ought to have tattooed on your eyeball. The fundamental strategy for managing uncertainty in any cause-and-effect process is the buffer. Buffers in network model schedules take the form of time padding. Thinking about a flow model might lead us to think about other kinds of buffers.

Every buffer is waste of some form or another, but some wastes are easier to control than others, and sometimes exchanging one waste for another is still an improvement to the whole. Schedule buffers represent the waste of delay. With a pull system, we might introduce small inventories to smooth out the flow between adjacent processes and reduce delays due to congestion.

A workflow buffer is a small inventory between two processes to create the appearance of instant availability to the downstream process. These buffers can be managed with kanban in the same way that other work-in-process is managed. Think about the stock on the shelf at the grocery store. When the shelf space is empty, this signals the grocer to replenish it. The inventory on the shelf can be very small if the grocer replenishes frequently. In fact, this is where the kanban idea comes from in the first place.

In a production process, a kanban buffer signals an upstream state to produce work only when there is actual demand for it. The productivity of downstream processes regulates the productivity of upstream processes, and this kind of regulation is called a *pull system*. At the moment a downstream process consumes a component from an upstream process, the upstream process begins production of a replacement. The kanban queue itself has a limit, so that if the queue fills up, the upstream producer will halt. The simple case is a queue limit of one.

The pipeline model forced process states to produce at the same rate and to release work at the exact moment that the next state needed it. By removing the synchronization clock, adjacent states can get out of step. Rate control can still be managed by setting WIP limits. The timing of work transfers can be managed by kanban buffers.

One of the nice things about not being a manufacturing process is that you are not constrained by the limits of physical space. Our kanban container can be infinitely large and occupy no space. Items can enter and exit in any order. In a manufacturing process, the kanban buffer will most likely be a first-in-first-out queue. A development workflow need not observe any such ordering. It might be advantageous to pick the dequeuing order according to local conditions visible to the people on the line.

However, controlling the size of the buffers is still very important. The ideal buffer size is 0, because all buffers are waste, but if a buffer is necessary for synchronization, then the ideal size is 1. If the buffer size grows much bigger than one, then you might consider adjusting downward the WIP limit of the upstream state instead. Remember that the only goal of the kanban buffer is to create the appearance of instant availability downstream.

There's another kind of inventory buffer that we might need to keep things flowing. Some resources may have natural batch sizes greater than one, or have less-than-immediate availability. We don't want to burden the upstream state with managing such a resource, so we can add a feeding buffer in front of the resource that still looks like a workflow buffer to the upstream state.

ARE WE THERE YET?

We had to take a stroll from the real through the imaginary in order to get back to the real again. But we are, in fact, back to reality, because the ideas described here are being applied by a growing number of software development teams in a variety of applications from software maintenance to new product development. And it works!

A perfect state of flow may be very difficult, or at least uneconomical, to achieve in a robust product development process. But we can get pretty close with a well-tuned kanban pull system. We have managed to combine most of the flexibility of craft production with most of the control of a pipeline. Work-in-process is limited, and cycle time can be managed. Most importantly, it is a highly transparent and repeatable process with all of the right conditions for continuous improvement. And continuous improvement is really what this is all about.

TIME-BOXED ITERATION: AN IDEA WHOSE TIME HAS COME AND GONE

Poor Winston Royce. The guy's big idea is vilified because of a popular *misunderstanding* of its meaning. The great irony of the Waterfall story is that Royce himself was trying to describe a more feedback-driven overlapping process.

But somehow, the Waterfall strawman itself became the reference model, presumably because it appealed to the authoritarian command-and-control mass-production paradigm of the American business culture of the 1970's. In a triumph of absurdity, that very culture was about to reach its nadir of quality, productivity, and profitability, as the dawn of an era of humiliating ass-kicking at the hands of the Japanese lean producers had just begun.

The contemporaneous emergence of the "structured" paradigm with all of its top-down orientation probably only encouraged the enthusiastically misguided technology managers of the day. After all, wasn't that the very promise of computer technology? That it would make predictions, automate production and accounting functions, provide managers with awesome new powers of control so that we didn't have to rely so much on those pesky, unreliable *workers* anymore?

Of course, many serious thinkers about software development were uneasy with that direction, because few of them ever thought of the problem that way in the first place. The phasist project management model was imposed from without by a zealous and out-of-control management culture, desperate to assert social dominance in the face of mounting economic failure.

Like any big new idea, the structured/phased paradigm took quite a long time to fully diffuse through the profession. Consequently, it also took quite a long time for the profession to come back with a well-formulated reaction. The most forceful expression of that reaction was probably Barry Boehm's Spiral Model.

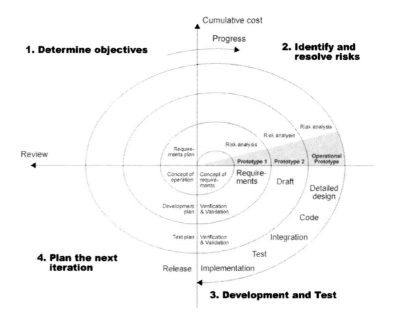

The Spiral Model was not the revolution, it was the counter-revolution, but the momentum of the Waterfall/SDLC was such that it took a decade for the Spiral to be fully realized as an enterprise-class methodology, in the form of the Rational Unified Process (RUP). Now, for those who were paying attention, the elements of RUP had been visibly gestating all the while, it just took some time to build up the fighting weight necessary to challenge the reigning champion. For the Object-Oriented faithful, it had always been a given that iterative development was the only credible approach.

The challenges before RUP were formidable. It had to simultaneously replace structured analysis/design methods *and* phased project management methods. But change was in the air, and the explosion of new technology and the resulting financial speculation suddenly made it look very uncool to hang on to yesterday's business processes. The dysfunction of phasist project management was abundantly clear to anybody who was paying even the slightest attention, so the world was finally ready for a credible contender. On the other hand, a generation of middle managers would never accept a methodology that threatened the corpulent bureaucracy that would allow them to rest and vest through a finance-fueled stock market orgy, so it was in everybody's best interest to make RUP as bloated and artifact-laden as possible. In this way, RUP was destined not to last, but it did serve to introduce a big idea into mainstream thought:

*Maybe 5 iterations of 100 requirements is better
than 1 iteration of 500 requirements.*

Just like the asteroid killed off the dinosaurs in order to make room for the birds and the mammals, the dotcom bubble accelerated the retirement of a generation of middle managers and left behind a world less hospitable to the flourishing of heavyweight processes. RUP's unwieldy bloatocracy had outlived its usefulness to the scrappy survivors of the Great IT Catastrophe of 2001. Furthermore, what you probably learned from executing 100 requirements in an iteration is that they have a funny way of multiplying into 200 requirements. Building 200 requirements at a time is not really that much more fun than building 500 requirements at a time, you just learn the truth a little faster (i.e. your budget is screwed and your quality will be awful).

Our faith in iteration remained undeterred, but something about the artifact-and-scope-driven approach of the 1990's was clearly not working. Fortunately, while the Object Establishment was busy making the enterprise safe for the Spiral Model, another group was determined to continue to drive the idea to a more extreme conclusion:

*Maybe 50 iterations of 10 requirements is better
than 5 iterations of 100 requirements.*

and furthermore:

> *If 10 requirements typically take a team 2 weeks,
> maybe 50 iterations of 2 weeks is better than 50
> iterations of 10 requirements.*

My experience (and I believe that of many others) with scope-driven coarse-grained iteration is that it does not work well. On the other hand, the enduring popularity of Agile time-boxed iteration in recent years suggests very strongly that it does work well. The wheels turn slowly, but perhaps the champions of iteration were right all along. But then, this mixed history suggests a troubling question: why does 10 work when 100 doesn't? What is a good size? What is the ideal size?

The answer to these questions takes us right back to the beginning of our story. Back when the software development world was first trying to recreate the obsolescent mass-production culture of its day, the Japanese had already provided us with the answer. The ideal batch size is one. Since 2004, I've been operating software development kanban systems with and without Agile-style iterations. My goal as a lean workcell manager has been the realization of one-piece flow. What I've learned from my experience is:

> *In a well-regulated pull system, iterations add no
> value at all.*

Just like RUP was a historical necessity to establish the legitimacy of the question, I believe that the first-generation Agile processes are a historical necessity to confirm that batch size is just as important to a development process as it is to a manufacturing process. And now that we know what the question really is, we find that we also know the answer. Iteration is only a transient concept to lead us to the deeper truths of *pull* and *flow*. The second generation of Agile processes will have no need for iterations as such. Continuous integration will be matched by continuous planning and continuous deployment. Live software systems will evolve before your eyes, and Little's Law will rule the world.

WORKFLOW

SCHEDULE IS ORTHOGONAL TO WORKFLOW

This is the essential principle that allows Lean development to be something more than Agile.

As a consequence of its minimalism, Scrum paves the way for post-Agile methodology. This might not be too surprising, given that Scrum is the closest to Lean thinking in its origin. Scrum differs somewhat from its Agile peers by refraining from specifying a workflow. It has been customary within the Scrum community to suggest that this workflow should be informal and self-organizing in the Agile tradition, but there's nothing within Scrum proper that mandates this informality. In fact, there's really nothing to stop you from using Scrum to schedule a more rigorous workflow like the SEI Personal Software Process ™.

What Scrum does require is that work requests should be small (a few person-days of effort), stated in terms of customer utility, and that once started, they will be completed to integration and acceptance testing. A fancier way of saying this is that Scrum requires *orthogonality of requirements*. If work requests must be independent of one another, and also independent of workflow, then we may also say that Scrum makes *schedule orthogonal to workflow*.

The method of Axiomatic Design demonstrates why orthogonality of requirements is a consequence of an ideal design. Regardless of the process used to produce a design, the ideal outcome of a design process is a system with functionally independent requirements

How convenient is it that an ideal design, by definition, *already satisfies the essential constraint for the ideal work scheduling algorithm*? Surely this cannot be a coincidence.

The revelation here is that a batch-and-queue phased process buys you *absolutely nothing* with respect to final design quality, but *does* impose deep inefficiencies on your business. Sounds like a great deal.

Batching and queuing are artifacts of assumptions in the implementation of process. There is nothing intrinsic to the SEI Team Software Process ™ that requires batching and queuing of requirements. Neither does the V Model. Nor is there any intrinsic batching to most of the Design for Six Sigma (DFSS) techniques.

The front end of requirements gathering will often deal in larger chunks, but the ideal output of requirements analysis should produce independently schedulable features. If it doesn't, then Axiomatic Design is already telling you that you've done something wrong.

The Agile movement has given us both big advances and big distractions. The good news is that we can toss out the distractions and substitute something better.

In this spirit, Lean Software Engineering will:

- **Develop** a deep characterization of **customer needs**, based on close customer interaction *and* sophisticated modeling tools;

- **Produce** finely grained, formally **specified requirements** that can be independently scheduled for development;

- **Follow** a rigorous and **formal engineering workflow** with multiple preventive quality control steps, and planned continuous process improvement;

- **Collect useful statistics** about quality and productivity as an integrated part of everyday work activities;

- **Continuously integrate** new features into a working, stable, secure, and reliable system; and

- **Make** those **new features available** to customers at every appropriate opportunity.

WORKFLOW EXAMPLES

Because of its simplicity, Scrum serves as a convenient reference model to discuss different workflows. For example, it has become somewhat common to use Scrum as the outer loop for the XP workflow. Scrum is not the only way to manage workflows, but its simplicity and familiarity make it useful for examples.

The executive summary of Scrum is:

- **Make plans** around fixed-duration iterations (typically 4 weeks);

- **Break** work **down** into small customer-valued features that can be delivered within one iteration;

- **Don't interrupt** the team in the middle of an iteration; and

- **Deliver** functional improvements to customers at the end of every iteration

Scrum doesn't say much about what happens between "small customer-valued features" and "deliver functional improvements," other than establishing criteria for inputs and outputs. The implication is:

> *Within the constraints of Scrum, use a development process that is most appropriate to your particular circumstance.*

One could imagine a particular circumstance where something very simple is sufficient:

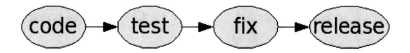

Now, is this ever a good practice? The answer is: *it depends.* What makes it a good practice or not is the production of an satisfactory outcome for the customer. For a sufficiently skilled developer writing for a limited audience with low criticality, it may very well be a sufficient process. It may be especially so if the developer is practicing a personal continuous improvement discipline, although you may think that would tend to take the form of improving the workflow.

One could also imagine a workflow that was very general. For instance, Deming's generic workflow is:

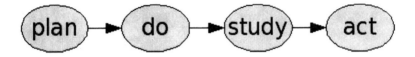

...where *Plan* might stand for the prioritization, analysis, estimation, scheduling, and resource allocation activities that are usually associated with software development. *Do* would correspond to design, coding, and verification. *Study* means analysis of the process that was applied in *Plan* and *Do*. *Act* means to make changes to that process based on what was learned in *Study*.

Study and *Act* together constitute the continuous improvement practice that is so central to the Deming philosophy. In fact, that Deming cycle is often discussed in the context of Scrum, giving us a clue about what sort of processes might be possible.

The historical context of Scrum aligns it with Agile methodology in general, so it is not surprising that it is frequently paired with the Extreme Programming (XP) workflow in order to define a complete process. The XP workflow looks roughly like:

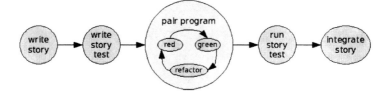

One very interesting thing about XP is the way it utilizes an explicit tight feedback loop to produce design specification and verification. If you unbundle the XP *pair programming + test-driven development* practice, you might get something like this fine-grained V model workflow:

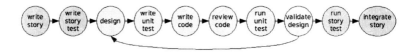

...which, as far as development workflows go, is not particularly novel.

If pair programming is not possible in your environment, then I think it is very helpful to deconstruct XP in this way in order to make more situationally appropriate choices. If you take out pair programming, the remaining unconventional notions are simply *story*, and backflow from *validate design* to *design*.

Story is already intrinsic to Scrum, which factors it out of our workflow consideration. Symmetric backflows are always implicit to the V model, but here we're making a stronger statement: *we expect to iterate our design and probably more than once.*

If we're doing Scrum + XP, and we decouple the XP workflow just a little, then suddenly a number of alternative workflows should be quite plausible. To see just how far we can go with that idea, let's consider something that many people would consider to be the polar opposite of Agile: The SEI Personal Software Process ™ (PSP).

Of course, there's much more to PSP than just the core development workflow. There is a considerable amount of design and estimation that PSP requires before coding can begin. We can assume that Scrum + PSP would include additional activities around project launch and iteration planning. But here, we're mostly interested in detailed development.

The PSP development workflow is something like:

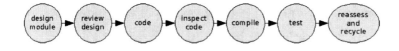

The obviously odd thing about this workflow is the placement of *inspect code* before *compile,* which is highly contrary to common contemporary practice and the exact opposite approach from XP.

Before you dismiss that idea, mature TSP/PSP teams measure code quality on a scale of defects per *million* lines of code[2], and the *inspect-before-compile* practice is a significant part of how this is accomplished. We also have the *reassess and recycle* step (much like the

Deming *study-act* steps), which adjusts the plan based on new data from the completed workflow. Unit test development and execution is considered implicit within design and test activities. Some of what makes PSP notorious is what happens *within* each workflow step, but the workflow itself is not too radical.

XP has an obvious fit with our Lean customer-value orientation, but PSP seems to be missing something in this regard. Few customers would ever care about delivery of something like a "module," so PSP must have some other activity that translates requirements into a design that includes things like modules. Pulling some part of that activity back into the inner development workflow would have to be the first modification we make to PSP to adapt it to our Lean scheduling discipline. Can we make such a change without compromising the high code quality that PSP promises?

The simple solution is to replace the *design module* step with a *design feature* step, where *feature* is defined as something small that has customer value and can be built and verified to full integration. Feature Driven Development provides a clear best practice on how to define such a thing.

A feature has the potential to cut across multiple modules, components, or even subsystems, so we need a way to control changes to dependent features. Refactoring and automated regression testing are part of how we will manage this, but we might need some extra power if we are to live up to PSP's extreme quality potential. Axiomatic Design can help us here by setting rules for how features should relate to one another and give us data about when which features need to be retested. We might insert a *validate design* step after *test feature* and use the design axioms, coupling metrics, and performance results to tell us when to iterate back to *design feature.*

It would be quite a stretch to include TSP/PSP or Axiomatic Design under the Agile umbrella, yet with a little help from FDD, we have little trouble fitting them into our Lean approach. This is how Lean is going to lead us forward. If we can adapt these very different off-the-shelf processes to work in a Lean fashion, can we improve them further or even develop our own custom workflow? Of course we can!

KANBAN WORKFLOW FOR PRODUCT DEVELOPMENT

ONE PIECE FLOW MEETS THE V MODEL

One-Piece Flow is what we call the Lean goal of pulling individual work requests through a sequence of value-adding activities quickly and without interruption. Flow addresses the wastes of transportation, overproduction, and inventory.

A *workcell* is a collection of production resources, organized according to the type of product made. This is in contrast to organizing resources by function or department. On the factory floor, functional organization might mean keeping all of the drills together and all of the ovens together. In the engineering office, this means keeping all of the analysts together and all of the testers together. Organizing by project vs. function is an old debate in project management, and the resolution usually falls under the category of *matrix organization*, which combines some features of both functional- and project-oriented structure, usually with one primary and one secondary hierarchy.

The *feature team* is one approach to matrix organization. A feature team is a situational workcell, where departmental resources are temporarily assigned to a small project team for the duration of that project's goal. Each feature team should contain most of the resources it needs to execute on its goal without requesting or waiting on resources from functional departments. This means that a feature team should be a cross-functional team, with a sufficient variety of expertise to complete its task with competence.

At the completion of the project goal, the feature team's resources should be returned to their departments for redeployment. Scrum and Microsoft's *feature crew* are explicitly feature team methods, but other Agile and iterative methods imply or at least allow for feature team organization.

One strength of the feature team is that it reduces the need for communication artifacts, which are analogous to transportation costs (i.e. documents transport process information between distant endpoints). Feature teams control overproduction by having limited and well defined scope and duration. Feature teams control inventory by making productive resources more available to work when there is work to be done. Feature teams, being workcells, are capable of *flow*.

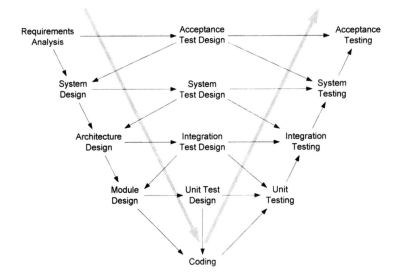

The *V Model* workflow addresses the waste of rework by emphasizing prevention over correction of defects. The V Model improves on the waterfall by coordinating verification and validation activities across early and late stages in the workflow. The V Model's greater scrutiny of requirements reduces the rework associated with ambiguous or untestable requirements. The traditional interpretation of the V Model still suffers from the other three wastes of a waterfall process (transportation, overproduction, and inventory), but we already have a remedy for these three wastes! If the V Model reduces rework, can it be combined with flow in order to reduce the wastes of transportation, overproduction, inventory, *and* rework? Yes, of course it can. If the feature team has a balanced skill set, uses pull scheduling internally, and follows a V workflow, then these four wastes can easily be minimized.

FLOW REQUIRES A LITTLE BIT OF SLACK, BUT TOO MUCH SLACK IS WASTE

Feature teams address many types of waste, but they may introduce a new type of waste of their own: *delay.*

A feature team workcell improves availability of functional resources by including that resource directly on the team. A balanced team will have a skill set in proportion to the time spent on each activity in that skill set. So, if a feature spends an average of two hours in development for every hour in test, then you could have two developers and one tester on your team and come out roughly in balance, assuming that 2:1 proportion stays somewhat uniform for the duration of the project. Since feature teams ought to be small in order to best realize their function, some ratios will be harder to realize. What if the average dev/test ratio is 5:2? Should your feature team now include 5 developers and 2 testers in order to be balanced? That efficiency might come at the expense of efficiency elsewhere on the team or in the business at large. Should you starve other projects of resources just so that you can hit your optimum resource ratio?

One solution is to redefine the functional boundaries of tasks so that their durations work out to more convenient ratios. So if 2 developers overproduce with respect to 1 tester, then give the developers more responsibility for executing testing tasks before transferring the work to the testing resource. Lean thinking is generally far more concerned that *the right work is being done at the right time than who is doing the work*.

Lean teams should think less rigidly about their roles than traditional departmentally-organized teams. That most certainly doesn't mean giving up the division of labor entirely. It only means thinking pragmatically about roles and realizing that having people with some overlapping skills is a good thing.

A KANBAN TOKEN IS A SIGNAL TO PULL VALUE THROUGH THE WORKFLOW

In a pull system, an upstream processing state does not deliver work until the downstream state asks for it. In order for work to really flow, intermediate work products should be ready for delivery immediately upon request. If the upstream process simply produced work at its own pace in anticipation of future demand, that would be inventory and possibly overproduction, which are waste. So there has to be a way for the upstream state to produce just enough work for the downstream state to keep busy without accumulating inventory.

The *kanban token* is a common technique for managing the transfer of work between steps in a workflow. Kanban just means sign, and it is usually some kind of token that is used to replace a work product with a request to make another work product. It might be a card, or a ping pong ball, an electronic message, or in our case, a post-it note. A feature team can use kanban tokens to synchronize production rates, so that downstream states are rarely waiting for upstream states to complete something. That still leaves the possibility of upstream states idling while waiting for the kanban token, but we have to take one more step to address that issue.

A kanban system for regulating workflow can be so effective that it obviates the need for the feature team entirely. In the software maintenance system that David Anderson deployed at Corbis, work requests were pulled directly through functional departments who have made capacity commitments to the workcell, but have not dedicated any particular individuals. The development manager might commit 4 developers to the workcell at any time, but not any specific developers, and not always the same developers. So there is a workcell of a defined size, but there is no team.

Kanban scheduling of a One-Piece Flow V Model workcell can reduce the wastes of rework, inventory, overproduction, transportation, and delay. Not bad for a process that's also fun to use in real life!

ORGANIZATION

GUIDED SELF-ORGANIZATION

Much of the recent thinking in software engineering management stems from the realization that industrial-age command-and-control management structures are ineffective when applied to skilled labor and high-value business problems. Such problems are given high value because by their very nature, they include uncertainty, risk, and complexity. The best strategies for managing uncertainty and risk usually involve decentralization of responsibility. The Agile management philosophy is organized almost entirely around this theme of decentralization.

Any vigorous philosophical movement will contain its provocateurs, and some parts of the Agile community seem to have openly embraced self-organization as a revolt against management. Prudent thinkers may wonder if the revolutionary wing of the movement has taken things too far, and that moderation is now called for. In this case, perhaps there is a middle way. Not every problem calls for seeking compromise, but the history of Lean thinking suggests that such a middle path is precisely what is needed.

We ask software developers to be subject matter experts, technology experts, design experts, and good team members simultaneously. It is already difficult enough to keep them consistently good at those things, while simultaneously keeping up with the eternal treadmill of technology and the inexhaustible impatience of customers. It is unreasonable to also expect them to be experts in organizational economics and design. At least, not right away.

What is really called for is partnership between management and the workforce. Management knows more about some things. Workers know more about other things. The best organization results from cooperation in service of a common interest.

Lean thinking is about optimizing the whole system. You must see the whole before you can optimize the whole, and this is not a trivial capability. A healthy organization will cultivate and employ a few experts who excel in that capacity. The workforce can benefit greatly from a beneficent advisor that understands process control and organizational economics, and who can also relate to the daily experience of the people who do the work. W. Edwards Deming is the archetype for such an advisor.

In the software profession, it is common to hear advice like: "only hire the best and let them figure it out." This sentiment is nearly as misguided as command-and-control and antithetical to Lean thinking. "Hire the best" is an elitist and ultimately lazy management philosophy. Comically, that attitude is often accompanied by an unwillingness to pay top dollar for such talent. But even if you could hire such a team, consider that a championship athletic team will almost always defeat an all-star team, because the quality of the relationships between qualified players is usually more important than the individual performances.

A lean production system can seem almost supernatural to an inexperienced observer. People, processes, and technology magically seem to appear at the right time, do exactly what is needed, and no more. Lean systems are highly ordered and regular at the same time that they are flexible and responsive. The system, and the people that operate it, possess deep knowledge about the workings of their processes. In a mass production system, knowledge is concentrated at the top. In a craft production system, it is concentrated at the bottom. A lean system distributes knowledge evenly throughout the entire system. This means that there are rules– sometimes a lot of rules. But it is not just about following rules. Lean workers know that the rules have a purpose. They probably know what that purpose is, because they probably created the rules themselves. Lean self-organization depends on rules that are based on principles. Correct understanding of those principles and the ability to see the whole are the purpose of a coach, process engineer, or sensei. Adopting Lean principles for a development organization probably means increasing operational sophistication to the degree that professional expertise is needed. Lean does not mean letting the inmates run the asylum.

The lean manager must also be adaptive. The manager must thoroughly understand the ends of the system and collaborate with the workforce to realize the means. Mass production assumes a division of knowledge from the superior to the inferior–highly educated industrial engineers versus interchangeable semi-skilled laborers. The division of knowledge in a lean system is generalist vs. specialist. The leader sees more of the operation of the system as a whole and has more detailed understanding of the goal. The worker understands more about the operation of his workstation and his technical specialties.

The lean distribution of knowledge means a more collaborative relationship between management and the workforce. Managers trust that the workers know best about their responsibilities. Workers trust that managers have the right goal and see the true relationships between the production processes. A lean manager should focus on outcomes. He should favor results over plans, guiding without prescribing, and directing without dictating. A lean manager should seek leverage by exploiting the tacit knowledge of the workers. A lean manager should know how to recognize a good outcome, and make reasonable accommodation of human preference and capability in pursuit of that outcome. Hold people accountable, don't tell them what to do, provide support for learning and improvement that enables people to solve problems for themselves. A lean manager is nurturing, but neither controlling nor coddling. Continuous improvement is always the glue that binds the social contract of the lean organization. Everybody is expected to improve, at all times.

DIVISION OF LABOR IN LEAN SOFTWARE DEVELOPMENT WORKFLOWS

Imagine we have team of three people, each working as generalists in an agile-style process. They are all qualified and competent workers, and correctly execute the process that they intend to follow. They break their work up into customer-valued features that each take a few days to complete through integration.

One developer is a true generalist. It takes her a couple of days to produce a testable functional specification and high-level design. It takes her a couple of days to produce a detailed design and working code. And it takes her a couple of days to verify and validate everything, from code correctness to functional acceptance.

Another developer is basically competent at all of these things, but he is a more stereotypically geeky programmer who can crank out high-quality code for most product features in a day, on average. It takes him a bit longer than the others to do the customer-facing part, usually about 4 days for analysis and high-level design. He's also a bit slower with the validation, because again, if it ain't writing code, he's just not that excited about it. And for all the time he spends on specs, they are still mediocre, which results in rework in spite of his good coding skills.

The third developer, by contrast, has a sharp eye for design and is very friendly and sympathetic to the business and the customers. He knows the business so well that most of his specs only take a day to write. He's a competent coder, but a bit old-school in his style and it takes him a bit longer with the current technology. Plus, his heart isn't quite in it the way it used to be. It takes him three days to develop good code that everybody will feel comfortable with. On the other hand, since his specs are so clean and thorough, and he has a good rapport with the business, the testing usually goes very smoothly in about two days, also (tied for) the best on the team.

The team, on average, produces features with a cycle time of 6.67 days per feature. Overall, each team member produces at a similar rate.

```
2d + 2d + 2d = 6d
4d + 1d + 3d = 8d
1d + 3d + 2d = 6d
-----------------
                20 days / 3 features
               = 6.67 days/feature
```

It is a one-piece flow (per developer), and everybody is always busy with his or her feature. Nobody ever has to wait to start a new feature. Other than the personal slack built into the task times, capacity utilization is high.

But imagine if this team of generalists were allowed to focus only on the skills that they were best at:

```
1d + 1d + 2d = 4d
1d + 1d + 2d = 4d
1d + 1d + 2d = 4d
-----------------
                12 days / 3 features
               = 4 days/feature
```

Same people, same features, 40% improvement in productivity...

...if only it were that simple, because there is also a cost here. If they organize themselves as a pipeline, then that pipeline becomes subject to the Theory of Constraints. If they apply Drum-Buffer-Rope, then the testing task sets the pace at 2 days.

That means the total cycle time per feature is:

2d + 2d + 2d = 6d

...still an improvement over the generalists, but only by 10% (!). On the other hand, capacity utilization is now low, because two people now spend half of their time idle, waiting for the drum. Since they are the same people who were cross-trained enough to work as generalists in the first example, can they do anything to speed up the testing process which has been otherwise unimproved? Surely the answer must be yes.

Suppose each of the first two developers spends an extra half of a day doing additional work to optimize the testing process, so that testing only takes 1.5 days to complete instead of two. Introducing a pipeline might also introduce a new communication cost, but imagine that the extra half-day spent by each of the first two developers is in collaboration on the two features they have in process, both communicating and optimizing testability.

The total labor expended is now 4.5 days per feature, but all of the idle time has been stripped out, so that the total cycle time per feature is also 4.5 days. That is a real 33% improvement in throughput. Same people, same features, same skills, 33% faster. It is only an example, but is it not a realistic example?

WHAT ABOUT TRAINING?

An enthusiastic and observant Agilist might, by this point, object that we could improve the productivity of the team in the first example by improving their skills with training. That is indeed true. We could provide such training, and it may very well yield improvement.

We could also provide training to the team in the second example, which might also yield improvement. What sort of improvement might we expect in each example?

The generalist model suggests that we help each team member improve their weak skills to bring them up to par with the rest of the team. In any model, there is something to be said for cross-training because it facilitates communication and allows the business to adapt to change. But investing in training to overcome weaknesses is a classic management mistake.

In *First, Break All the Rules*, Buckingham and Coffman make a compelling and well-researched case that the best return on investment in training comes from enhancing a worker's strengths, rather than overcoming his weaknesses. The geeky coder may have a lack of charm or graphic design sensibility that no amount of training can ever overcome, but picking up a new coding technique or web application framework might pay immediate dividends.

The more specialized team has another built-in advantage in training because they simply get more practice with their currently deployed skills. The analyst gets more training on analysis, which he already has an aptitude for *and* then gets to spend all of his time practicing.

Back to our first team, imagine that we invest in generalist training, so that our

```
2 + 2 + 2 = 6
1 + 3 + 2 = 6
4 + 1 + 3 = 8
```

becomes

```
2 + 2 + 1 = 5
1 + 2 + 2 = 5
3 + 1 + 3 = 7
```

...for an improved average cycle time of $(5+5+7)/3 = 5.67$ days per feature. That would be a generous result in training, for a significant outcome.

What about our "invest in strengths" scenario for the first team?

```
2   + 2   + 1 = 5
0.5 + 3   + 2 = 5.5
4   + 0.5 + 3 = 7.5
```

...not as good! Even with a very generous 50% improvement for all, we only get 6 days per feature. What about the specialized team? If our original:

$$1 + 1 + 2 = 4$$

becomes

$$0.5 + 0.5 + 1 = 2$$

...and then we add back some collaboration overhead:

$$1 + 1 + 1 = 3$$

...well, then we are just smoking the generalist team. These are contrived examples, but they should still illustrate some of the advantages that go to small lean teams over small craft teams. The most effective teams have complementary skills and personalities, not homogeneous ones. Otherwise, why organize into teams at all?

STILL NOT THAT SIMPLE? ENTER THE KANBAN

A problem with both examples is that they deal with average features. However, nobody ever actually works on an average feature. They work on real features that can be averaged over time. Those features have variation, and sometimes a lot of it.

For this reason (and others), we don't organize our workflow by role. We organize it by task or process, and let team members apply themselves to the workflow in the most efficient manner. They may even hand off the work at different transitions depending on the feature or the state of the pipeline. Such a soft division of labor preserves the efficiency advantage of each worker, while also allowing for variation and changes in circumstance. What matters most is that the work is done in the right order by the best resource available at the time, not who does what.

Pooling work-in-process according to the kind of asynchronous kanban system we've been discussing smoothes out the flow of variable-duration work items, so that some of the variation in cycle times between processes is traded off for variation in inventory. Such a pooling strategy works better with more people than our examples, and also more people than the current common practice for agile teams. For a pipelined kanban system, we think that about 20 people is the sweet spot.

STARTING A KANBAN SYSTEM

EVOLUTION OF A LEAN DEVELOPMENT PROCESS

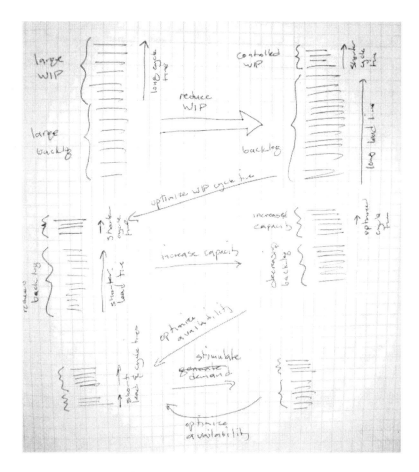

I scrawled this in a notebook at the Tully's Coffee in Wallingford in the winter of 2005, but it still seems about right. I was working through the steps for introducing a lean development process. That is, there's no magic wand that you can wave over your team to make them lean, and you can't do everything all at once. You have to start somewhere, and that somewhere is: *match your current work-in-process to your current capacity*. Of course, your current capacity will be defined by whatever you have the least of. Shorthanded on testers? Analysts? Your first step is to subordinate your current work-in-process to that resource. Only then can you begin a controlled and systematic expansion of your productive capacity.

START WITH SOMETHING SIMPLE

Process change is a difficult business. People get attached to their habits and tribal affiliations. People resist changes that threaten their social status. Effective process change addresses human issues of fear and hope before interfering with workers' routines. Deming and the Lean thinkers have much to say about this. One thing you can do is to take an evolutionary approach and keep changes small and incremental whenever possible. Sometimes disruptive changes are truly necessary, but they are also risky and should be treated as such.

I am deeply skeptical of any methodology that requires you to send the team off for training for any significant amount of time before deploying the process. If that is a precondition for success, then you should brace yourself for failure. If you have to make a big, discontinuous change, it should be done quickly and decisively, and facilitated by experts on site. If you know where you want to go, and there is a smooth and incremental path to get there, then you should follow it.

If you are starting from a phased, waterfall-type process and you have functionally-aligned teams, then you might start with a kanban process. If you have more project-aligned teams, then you might start with Scrum or feature crews.

If you are already using Scrum, Feature Crews, Feature Driven Development, Extreme Programming, or something similar, then you can use that as a starting point. As long as you are consuming customer-valued work and following through to continuous integration, then you have a foundation to build from. From here you could tackle the front end, upgrade to a kanban process, or you could upgrade your core engineering workflow. Let's assume that we're doing the latter for now.

Since Extreme Programming gives us a nice concrete model to work from, let's start there. If you can read between the lines of all of the rhetoric of XP, then you might see that it's a scaled down implementation of a V Model workflow. Most of the individual XP practices are concrete implementations of specific V Model states. The notion of the "irreducible interdependency" of practices is a faith-building tactic that is not supported by evidence. Once you start to look at it that way, you may then feel emboldened to substitute those practices with alternative practices that serve the same function with respect to the V Model.

For example, Test Driven Development, if it is done well, is very much like Design by Contract. Given the right tools, Design by Contract is, in turn, a form of formal specification. E.W. Dijkstra's 1976 book, *A Discipline of Programming*, describes the design process of *Correctness by Construction*, which is very clearly the origin of both TDD and Design by Contract (DbC). I tend to think of TDD as a method for the formal specification novice, so if you're looking for an opportunity to upgrade your practice, implementing Design by Contract would be an excellent start. And remember, the way to do DbC right is *write your postconditions first!*

You could also replace Pair Programming with the Capture/Recapture Code Inspection. You could insert Pugh Concept Selection before coding. You could insert Failure Modeling and Threat Modeling before Acceptance Testing. You could add multiple integration stages and insert more structural system testing. You can do any or all of these things (and more) as needed.

But first, if you are practicing Extreme Programming today, please stop thinking of it as Extreme Programming and start thinking of it as Lightweight Lean V Model with Practice Set { Onsite Customer, TDD, Pair Programming, ... }.

SCRUM-BAN

As more people become interested in Lean ideas and their application to knowledge work and project management, it is helpful to find ways that make it easier to get started or learn a few basic concepts that can lead to deeper insights later. For those that are curious about kanban in an office context, it is not unusual to find people who are either currently using Scrum, or have some understanding of Scrum as representative of Agile thinking. One way or another, Scrum users are an important constituent of the kanban audience. Since Scrum can be described as a statement in the language we use to describe kanban systems, it is also fairly easy to elaborate on that case in order to describe Scrum/ kanban hybrids. This can be useful for existing Scrum teams who are looking to improve their scale or capability. It can also be useful for more cautious new users who find comfort in an "established" method.

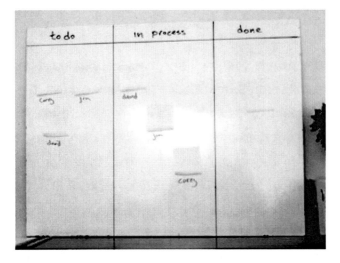

The idea of using a simple task board with index cards or sticky notes is as old as Agile itself. A simple variation of this is a task board with a simple *Pending -> In Process -> Complete* workflow. The cards represent work items in the current scope of work. Names can be associated with the cards to indicate who's working on what. Agile teams have been using this sort of method for a long time, and a few people pointed out early on that this had some resemblance to the notion of kanban in lean systems.

Of course, a variety of electronic tools exist that perform these functions, but the simple task board represents a couple of lean principles that I find very valuable, *simple technology* and *visual control*. The utility of such a simple method of workflow management is that it is easy to manage, and more importantly, *it is easy to change*. Huddling around a computer monitor, even a very large one, is in no way a substitute for the tactile and social interactivity that accompanies manipulating a large task board. Maybe someday it will. Not today. What electronic tools are good for are managing lists of things, like backlogs and bugs, and producing reports. Simple tools can be a difficult concept to explain to technology fanatics, but then, so can *value*.

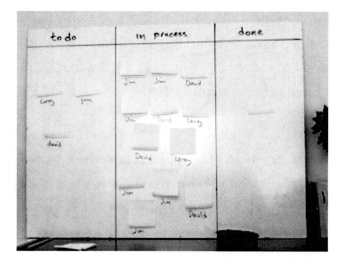

A problem with the basic index-card task board is that there is nothing to prevent you from accumulating a big pile of work in process. Time-boxing, by its nature, sets a bound on how much WIP that can be, but it can still allow much more than would be desirable. If a kanban is a token that represents a work request, and our task board can still get out of control, then what is the problem here? The problem is that a kanban is more than just a work request on a card, and putting sticky notes on a whiteboard is not enough to implement a pull system.

CRUNCHY ON THE OUTSIDE, CHEWY ON THE INSIDE

Just as an unregulated index card on a cork board is not
a kanban, time-boxed iteration planning is not pull. No
reasonable interpretation of Lean involves building to a
one-month forecast unless the cycle time for each work
order is also a month. One month worth of stuff in
process is certainly a much smaller batch size than 3
months or 18 months, but if your iteration backlog
contains 20 work items, then that's still about 19 more
than it needs to be a pull system.

Nonetheless, it is not difficult to augment Scrum with a
few simple practices that move us towards a more
recognizably lean workflow. The most obvious is the
reduction of iteration length, although this is not without
problems. As we'll see, it is possible to incrementally
enhance Scrum with more and more pull-like features
until all that remains of the original process is vestigial
scaffolding. The simple approach is to start with Scrum-
like iterations and iteration planning process, and begin
to add pull features to the team's internal process.

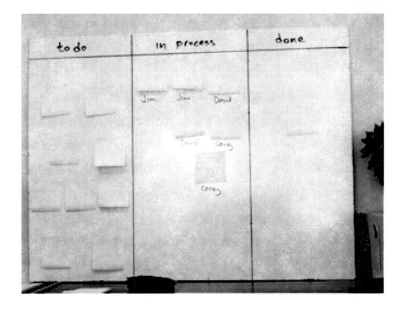

One simple technique that brings us much closer to our kanban definition is to set a multitasking limit for individuals. You might have a simple principle like: *prefer completing work to starting new work,* or you might express that as a rule that says: *try to work on only one item at a time, but if you are blocked, then you can work on a second item, but no more.* In our example, that rule gives our team of 3 an effective WIP limit of 6.

Another common technique is the late binding of tasks to owners. Some teams will pre-assign all of the known tasks during iteration planning. That's generally not a good idea because it artificially creates a critical path. Waiting until the "last responsible moment" to assign tasks to people maximizes knowledge and brings you closer to pull.

Just because *anybody* can have more than one item in
process doesn't mean that *everybody* should have more
than one item in process. A problem with our
multitasking rule is that it locally optimizes with no
consideration of the whole. An implicit total WIP limit of
6 is still more WIP than we should probably tolerate for
our three workers. A limit of 4 of 5 total items in process
at one time still allows for some multitasking exceptions,
but disallows the obviously dysfunctional behavior of
everybody carrying two items. At this step, we have
moved beyond a rule about individuals and have made a
rule about the task cards themselves. That is, we have
made our cards into kanban.

Another enhancement we can make to our previous board is to add a ready queue between the backlog and work-in-process. The ready queue contains items that are pending from the backlog, but have high priority. We still haven't bound any individual to these tasks, but as soon as somebody becomes available, they should take one of these tasks instead of picking something out of the general backlog. This enables us to decouple the process of assigning work from the process of prioritizing work, and it simplifies assignment. The ready queue also has a kanban limit, and it should be a small limit, since its only purpose is to indicate which work item should be started next.

Now we can begin to see some of the mechanics of pull and flow:

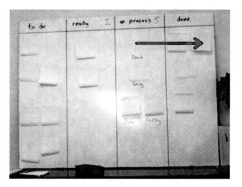

1. DAVID COMPLETES A TASK AND MOVES IT INTO THE "DONE" COLUMN.

2. DAVID PULLS A NEW KANBAN FROM THE READY QUEUE AND BEGINS WORKING.

3. THE TEAM RESPONDS TO THE PULL EVENT AND SELECTS THE NEXT PRIORITY ITEM
TO GO INTO THE READY QUEUE.

At this point, we are now operating a simple kanban pull system. We still have our time-boxed iteration and planning cycle, so perhaps we might call such a thing a Scrumban system!

Now that we have a sense of capacity and pull, it is natural to think about flow. Breaking up our nebulous "in process" state into better defined states can give everybody more visibility into the strengths, weaknesses, and overall health of the team. Even Agile workflows like Extreme Programming have relatively well-defined roles and states, and a smooth flow of work between those states is just as important as a smooth flow of work through the process overall.

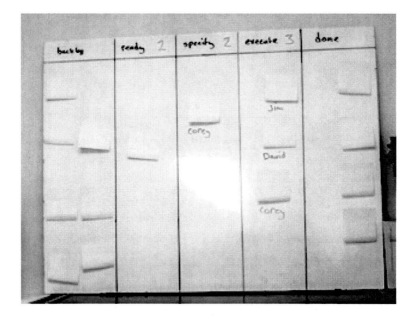

Here we've broken down *in-process* into two states: *specify* and *execute*. Specify is defining whatever criteria are necessary to determine when the work item can be considered complete. Execute is doing the work necessary to bring that work item into a state which satisfies those criteria. We have split our previous WIP limit of 5 across these two states. Specify is considered to take less time in this case, so it is given a limit of 2. Execute consumes the remaining limit of 3. We might change this ratio as time goes on and our performance changes.

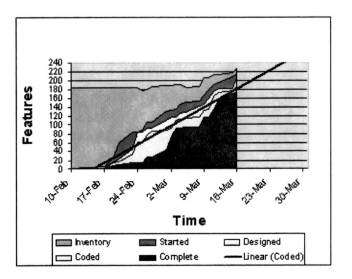

Since we are now thinking more about flow, the additional workflow detail strongly suggests using a Cumulative Flow Diagram (CFD) to track the work and measure our performance. A simple burndown tells you something about whether or not you are delivering value, but not very much about why. The CFD communicates a lot of additional information about lead times and inventories that can diagnose problems or even prevent them.

By defining our workflow a little better, we can also account for some functional specialization. In this case, it might be a soft specialization, where some of us prefer doing one type of work more than another, even though we're capable of doing it all. It is important to understand that this kind of pull workflow system *allows* specialization but does not *enforce* specialization. The team owns the work and the workflow, and it is up to the team to figure out how to get it done efficiently.

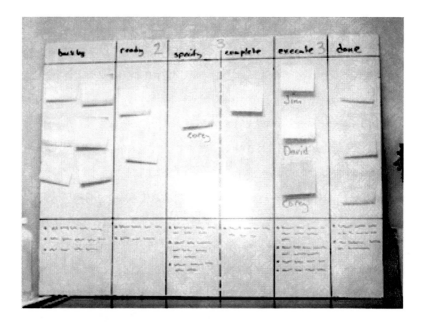

If we let the person who is best at performing the "specify" function handle more of that work, then we may also need to coordinate handoffs between ourselves. Adding the *specify-complete* column communicates to the team that a work item which was previously in the specify state is now ready to be pulled by anyone who wants to move it to the execute state. Work that is still in the specify state is not eligible to be pulled yet. If the owner of a ticket in the specify state wants to hand it off, he can put it in the complete buffer. If he doesn't want to hand it off, he can move it directly into the execute state as long as capacity is available. It might be that the execute state is full, and the only eligible work is to pull another ticket from the ready queue into specify.

Since we have added a new column for our handoff buffer, we are also increasing the WIP limit by a small amount. The tradeoff is that the increase in lead time due to the new inventory should be offset by the decrease in lead time due to the advantage of specialization. We also mitigate the impact of that new inventory by pooling the WIP limit across the preceding state. This has the very beneficial consequence of making the specify-complete buffer a variable throttle for the preceding station. The more work that piles up in the specify-complete buffer, the less work can be in process in the specify state, until specify is shut down entirely. But we see it coming; it doesn't "just happen."

If we're going to allow workflow specialization and the handoffs that result, then we will also need some agreement about what results to expect at each handoff. We can do that by defining some simple work standards or standard procedures for each state. These do not have to be complicated or exhaustive. Here, they are simple bullets or checklists drawn directly on the task board. They only need to be sufficient to avoid misunderstanding between producers and consumers. These standards are themselves made and owned by the team, and they can change them as necessary according the practice of *kaizen*. Putting them in a soft medium like a whiteboard or a wiki reinforces the notion of team ownership.

LEVEL 2 SCRUMBAN

In the basic version of Scrumban described so far, the iteration review and planning cycle happens just as it does in ordinary Scrum. But as our production process has matured, we have also given ourselves some tools to make the planning process more efficient, more responsive, and better integrated with the business that it serves.

With the pull system in place, our flow will become smoother as our process capability improves. We can use our inter-process buffers and flow diagrams to show us our process weaknesses and opportunities for kaizen. As we get closer to level production, we will start to become less concerned with burndown and more concerned with cycle time, as burndown is the effect and cycle time is the cause.

Average lead time and cycle time will become the primary focus of performance. If cycle time is under control and the team capacity is balanced against demand, then lead time will also be under control. If cycle time is under control, then burndowns are predictable and uninteresting. If burndowns are uninteresting, then goal-setting and risky heroic efforts are unnecessary. If burndowns are uninteresting, then iteration backlogs are just inventory for the purpose of planning regularity and feeding the pull system. As such, they should be the smallest inventories possible that optimize planning cost.

Since the team now pulls work into a small ready queue before pulling it into WIP, then from the team's perspective, the utility of the iteration backlog is that it always contains something that is worth doing next. Therefore, we should use the least wasteful mechanism that will satisfy that simple condition.

A simple mechanism that fits the bill is a size limit for the iteration backlog. Rather than go through the trouble of estimating a scope of work for every iteration, just make the backlog a fixed size that will occasionally run to zero before the planning interval ends. That's a simple calculation. It is just the average number of things released per iteration, which in turn is just a multiple of average cycle time. So if you have 5 things in process, on average, and it takes 5 days to complete something, on average, then you'll finish 1 thing per day, on average. If your iteration interval is two work weeks, or 10 work days, then the iteration backlog should be 10. You can add one or two for padding if you worry about running out. This might be a point that's been lost on the Scrum community: *it is never necessary to estimate the particular sizes of things in the backlog*. It is only necessary to estimate the average size of things in the backlog. Most of the effort spent estimating in Scrum is waste.

In our final incarnation of Scrumban, iteration planning still happens at a regular interval, synchronized with review and retrospective, but the goal of planning is to fill the slots available, not fill all of the slots, and certainly not determine the number of slots. This greatly reduces the overhead and ceremony of iteration planning. Time spent batch processing for iteration planning estimation can be replaced with a quality control inspection at the time that work is promoted to the ready queue. If a work item is ill-formed, then it gets bounced and repeat offenders get a root cause analysis.

OFF WITH THE TRAINING WHEELS

If you make it this far in your evolution, you will probably realize that the original mechanisms of Scrum are no longer doing much for you. Scrum can be a useful scaffold to hold a team together while you erect a more optimized solution in its place. At some point you can slough off the cocoon and allow the pull system to spread its wings and take flight.

The first step beyond Scrum is to decouple the planning and release periods. There may be a convenient interval to batch up features to release, and there may be a convenient interval to get people together to plan. If we have a leaner, more pull-driven planning method, there's no reason why those two intervals should be the same. Your operations team might like to release once a month, and your product managers might like to establish a weekly prioritization routine. No reason not to accommodate them.

Once you've broken up the timebox, you can start to get leaner about the construction of the backlog. Agility implies an ability to respond to demand. The backlog should reflect the current understanding of business circumstances as often as possible. In other words, the backlog should be event-driven. Timeboxed backlog planning is just that, where the event is a timer, and once we see it that way, we can imagine other sorts of events that allow us to respond more quickly to emerging priorities. Since our system already demonstrates pull and flow, that increased responsiveness should come at no cost to our current efficiency.

The problem we are trying to solve is:

The ideal work planning process should always provide the development team with best thing to work on next, no more and no less.

Further planning beyond this does not add value and is therefore waste. Scrum-style timeboxed planning usually provides a much bigger backlog than what is strictly necessary to pick the next work item, and as such, is unnecessary inventory and therefore unnecessary waste.

The next event we might consider for scheduling planning activities is the concept of an *order point*. An order point is an inventory level that triggers a process to order new materials. As we pull items from the backlog into the process, the backlog will diminish until the number of items remaining drops below the order point. When this happens, a notice goes out to the responsible parties to organize the next planning meeting. If our current backlog is 10, our throughput is 1/day, and we set an order point at 5, then this planning will happen about once a week.

Once a week might be reasonable if people are hard to
schedule or need some lead time in order to prioritize.
However, if they are more available than that, then we
can set the order point lower. If the planners can
respond within a day, then perhaps we can set the order
point at 2. If the order point is 2, then there may be no
need to keep a backlog of 10. Perhaps we can reduce
the backlog to 4...and reduce our lead time by 6 days in
the process.

The end state of this evolution is pull, or prioritization-
on-demand. If the planners can make a good decision
quickly enough, and there is no economy of scale in
batching priority decisions together, then the size of the
backlog only needs to be 1. At the moment the item is
pulled by the development team, the planning team is
signaled to begin selecting the next item. If the planning
team is fast enough in its response, then the
development team will never stall. If there is some
variation or delay in response, then a backlog of 2 might
be necessary to prevent stalls. But 2 is still a lot smaller
and leaner than 10. Or 20. Or 50, which is something
I've seen more often than I would like.

The same kind of logic can be applied to the release
interval. There is an optimum batch size for releases and
we should first try to find it, and then try to improve it.
The result of our efforts will ultimately be features-on-
demand.

Even at this level, we still have a fairly basic kanban system. From here we can add work item decomposition (swimlanes), or structural dependency flow for additional scale. Along with an enlightened division of labor, this is how we believe that Lean shows the way to scale Agile up to the enterprise.

KANBAN BOOTSTRAP

The goal of a kanban workflow system is to maximize the throughput of business-valued work orders into deployment. It achieves this by regulating the productivity of its component subprocesses.

I bootstrapped one such kanban system for an enterprise software project in the Autumn of 2007. It was a large project, with more than 50 people directly participating. Starting up a new project means making predictions about workflow states, resource allocation, productivity, work item size, priority criteria, and so on.

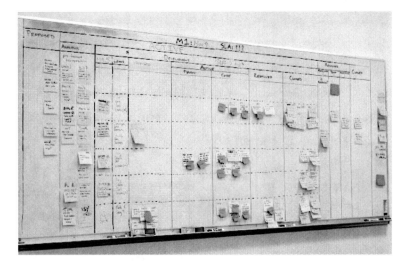

This project is too large for a single pipeline, so we have a nested structure that processes incoming scope in two stages. The first breakdown (green tickets) is by business-valued functional requirements that can be covered by a small functional specification and corresponding test specification. The second stage (yellow tickets) breaks down these "requirement" work packages into individual "features" that can be completed through integration by an individual developer (or pair) within a few days. The outer workflow is fed by a Rolling Wave project plan, but the flow itself is expected to be continuous. Scope decomposition is generally as "just-in-time" as is tolerable to the stakeholders.

Only time and real live performance data can tell you what you need to know to configure such a process correctly. It takes a while to move enough work through the system in order to obtain sufficient data to set the right process parameter values.

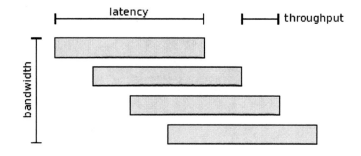

Until then, you have to keep a sharp eye on things and engage in a lot of speculation about coming events. A particular challenge is with measuring latency. Latency can be a much bigger value than throughput. Worse, latency at the beginning of a big project is likely to be much worse than its stable value. New people working on a new project using a new process make for abundant sources of variation with both special and common causes. You have to see through all of this early noise in order to estimate the implied stable latency. Then you can get down to the hard work to make the worst of that variation go away, and buffer for the rest.

In comparison, bandwidth is easy to manipulate. For a stable process, adjusting bandwidth can have a relatively immediate impact on performance. But at the beginning, you can do little but help push that first order through the system as quickly as possible. You have to prime the pump, and that is a different problem than regulating flow.

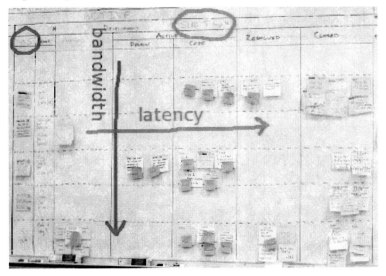

The trouble with estimating bandwidth is that you won't know if you are correct until you can measure latency. Overshooting bandwidth might result in a traffic jam in a downstream process that will stretch out your lead time. Undershooting bandwidth will result in "air bubbles" flowing through the process that confound your ability to configure downstream resources that are also ramping up.

The pressure is to overshoot. Everybody who's available to work thinks that they ought to dive in and start hammering away. It's hard to tell people to wait for the pull when there's nothing to pull but slack. You have to imagine what the rate of pull is going to be, adjust the input valve accordingly, and try to get people to contribute anything they can towards reducing latency. If there is ever a good time to employ pair programming, this is it. But then, that's just one more thing you have to try to convince people to do. When they've been champing at the bit, everybody wants their own piece of the pie.

Until you have meaningful throughput measurements, you have to make hands-on adjustments to bandwidth based on the live behavior of the workflow. If you see the traffic jam forming, close the valve. If you see the air bubble forming, open it up. Later you can let a well-sized buffer absorb the random variation without intervention.

Given the choice, I would always start one of these projects with a small pilot team. I'd let the workflow latency stabilize before ratcheting up bandwidth. Otherwise, there's just too much variation to control without exceptional effort. Alas, it can be difficult to explain why you should idle available resources in order to stabilize your process while the cold, hard wind of calendar time is blowing in your face.

KANBAN FLOWING ACCORDING TO ARCHITECTURE

So far, we've been discussing kanban systems aligned according to workflow. We've found that this scales up to teams of about 50 people, beyond which we worry about team cohesion. For larger problems, we will have to introduce new elements of organizational structure.

It is natural to represent workflows as state machines, and we have already introduced hierarchical state machines in progressively decomposing functional specifications into 'features'.

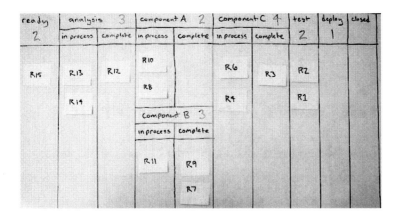

At the next level of scale, imagine an architecture that is partitioned into three components: two lower-level components that are largely independent of one another, and a higher-level component that integrates features from the other two:

Perhaps it is a web application that consumes two web services. Each component has a work-in-process (WIP) limit and a completion queue. Each component may internally manage its own WIP using a workflow kanban system, so that the "in process" state for component A explodes into a separate board like the one at the top.

Suppose each of the yellow tickets represents a 20-page functional specification. Each of those specs might be broken into 20 features. Component A has 15 people assigned, B has 20, C has 25, and there are another 20 assigned to the system overall, for a total of 80 people.

The WIP limits of components A and B are proportioned according to the rate of consumption by component C. The relative rate of consumption of A or B may shift over time, and WIP limits can be adjusted up or down in response.

Imagine in this case that C is under its limit in spite of available capacity. They are waiting on an interface from A. A is at its limit, and does not have capacity to spare. This might be an isolated occurrence, but if it happens often, then resources might be allocated to A, or A might work on improving its cycle time. At the same time, B seems to be working ahead a little, so maybe B can reassign some people to A to help them along, Brooks' Law notwithstanding. Test might be a little backed up, but they are relieved by slack in C.

For a well-factored architecture, this kind of system should scale out to hundreds of people.

RUNNING A KANBAN SYSTEM

KANBAN DAILY STANDUP MEETINGS

The daily work planning meeting is a unifying theme across Agile methods. The daily standup meeting has become a cultural fixture in development shops around the world.

The conventional standup meeting focuses on relationships between team members. The Daily Scrum enumerates the project participants for a brief status report. The theory behind this is that communication costs become the limiting factor to productivity as projects grow in complexity. The Daily Scrum ensures that an n-way information exchange happens at least once per day. It also bounds this cost by limiting the duration of the meeting, usually 15 minutes, and by imposing rules on the format. If further discussion is required, it can be conducted after the meeting between the interested participants. The time limit of the meeting also limits the number of possible participants. A Scrum team is necessarily limited to fewer than 10 people, because its practices do not scale well beyond that size. A project that requires a larger team will be split into sub-teams that fit the Scrum limits.

A kanban pull system is more focused on work and workflow than the first-generation Agile processes. Nowhere does this difference in emphasis show more clearly than in the daily standup meeting. Kanban projects have no trouble scaling up to 40 or more people with work assignments on the *heijunka* board. The comfort zone appears to be about 25 people. That number seems to strike a good balance between comfort and efficiency. 50 people certainly has a more authoritarian tone than 20, but it can still be manageable. Beyond that, it is probably best to divide into parallel workcells. There are real economies of scale to be had with a unified team, so splitting up should not be done until the team shows signs of inefficiency or discomfort.

Now, 30 people could not possibly all give a meaningful status report in 15 minutes. Nevertheless, our kanban teams complete their standups in 15 minutes with great reliability and satisfactory results. So, they must be doing something different.

The major difference in a kanban standup is that the meeting facilitator enumerates work, not people. There is an ongoing expectation that workstations will pull an available work request any time they have capacity at the station. People who are available and eligible to operate a workstation are expected to attach to any stations that have capacity according the board. People are expected to do this on their own initiative, rather than wait for assignment at the standup. If the standup facilitator sees openings on the board, she may prompt the team to assign the work and then issue a stern word to pay more attention!

The facilitator should strive to create a motivating, coaching atmosphere in the meeting. People in the room should adopt a tactical planning mentality during the meeting, looking for problems to address and opportunities to facilitate flow.

The meeting format assumes that the process is correct and that work-in-process is flowing through it. If everything is going well with a work item, then there may be nothing to discuss. The focus should be on exceptions. Status will be queried for existing issues on the board. The facilitator will ask a few leading questions to identify any new issues with work-in-process. If anybody feels that his or her work is blocked, then an issue should be created and tracked. If any detailed discussion of an issue is required, then it should be conducted after the meeting between interested parties. Encourage the team to express irritation with detailed conversations about topics that do not concern them.

When enumerating the work, it is useful to traverse the board from right-to-left, or downstream-to-upstream, in order to emphasize pull. As you trace out the flow of work-in-process, there may be some planning discussion to prepare downstream operators for the work that will be coming their way shortly. Sometimes clever tactical decisions can be made that will optimize the overall flow of work through the system.

STRIKING A DIFFERENT BARGAIN WITH THE BUSINESS

Iteration planning is another core element of Scrum. Scrum divides the calendar into fixed-duration time boxes. Traditionally, this is 4 weeks, though some teams make it shorter. Scrum aims to limit disruption of work-in-process by the business, so the 4 week iteration cycle includes a planning window where the business is allowed (expected, even) to adjust the content of a backlog of pending work requests. Of the prioritized backlog, the team estimates the scope of work it believes it can deliver in the iteration and sets a goal to do so.

The bargain with the business is that the stakeholders have a time to have their say, but otherwise are expected to leave the team alone to complete its goal. In a nutshell, Scrum's expectation of the business is:

You may not interrupt work in process, and you
may not adjust the work plan more frequently than
once every n days.

Our teams strike a different bargain with the business:

You may not interrupt work in process, and you
*may not adjust the work plan **less** frequently than*
once every n days.

But...if the business can come in and change priorities any time it likes, how can you commit to a goal?

A scope-driven goal is only one kind of goal. We don't make that kind of goal. Another kind of goal is quality of service, and that is what we do. The team commits to deliver working features, on average, within a time limit that we consider a Service Level Agreement, or SLA. A typical SLA for us would be something on the order of 30 days. The engineering team's promise is:

When we agree to take on a work request, we
intend to deliver it within n days.

According to this criterion, it doesn't really matter what the work is in the backlog. It only matters that the work has been appropriately sized and has been specified with a reasonable amount of clarity. This also greatly simplifies estimation by setting a single sizing criterion: *not too big to meet the SLA*. And if you don't make a scope-driven goal, then there's no such goal to meet and no need to package any such group of features together for delivery.

So we don't do that either.

What we do instead is agree to release all of the features that have been completed since the prior release on a periodic interval. Because the amount of work that is in process is limited, that means that the rate of features exiting the process has to be the same as the rate of features entering the process. Some features are bigger, and some features are smaller, but on average, most releases will be of a similar size.

This kind of arrangement means that the planning interval and the release interval don't have to be the same, which means that there are no time boxes and no iterations. The planning interval should be often enough to keep the input queue from starving. The release interval should be set to the optimum point between the cost of deploying a new release vs. the opportunity cost of carrying finished inventory. If the cost to release is high, you'll want to release less often. If the cost to release is low, you'll want to release more often. Cost of release is a worthy target to optimize and the ideal result is deployment on demand.

THROUGHPUT, LEAD TIME, AND DEMING

We can use a quality-of-service goal to manage the performance of our development process. The underlying goal of the process is throughput, by which we mean the rate of delivery of customer-valued work into production. The two major variables that regulate throughput are work-in-process and cycle time. We manage WIP very closely using limits and visual control.

Cycle time is a bit more difficult to manage, because this is where most of the variation manifests. Here, we have a number of capabilities that we can apply to reducing variation, including:

- analysis practices that accurately identify work items that are too large

- engineering practices that reduce rework due to preventable causes

- high visibility into blocking issues and active management of those issues

I say we have a quality-of-service goal, but "goal" might be the wrong word. As Deming said:

> *Eliminate slogans, exhortations, and targets asking for zero defects or new levels of productivity. Such exhortations only create adversarial relationships, as the bulk of the causes of low quality and low productivity belong*

to the system and thus lie beyond the power of the work force.

Eliminate numerical goals, numerical quotas, and management by objectives. Substitute leadership.

So, the importance of the lead time SLA is not in its motivational value. What's important is that its value is under control. Therefore, there are always two phases of setting a numerical limit like our SLA:

1. Bring the system into a state of control. Whatever the control limit is, does the system perform consistently with respect to that limit? If not, identify the sources of variation that cause divergence and find a way to manage them.

When it does stabilize...

2. ...change something about the system in order to improve its performance. This may throw the system out of control for a while, which will focus your attention back on (1).

If you only randomly make your target, or consistently miss the target, then the problem is that the target is wrong, not the process. Proper management action is to identify a new target and stabilize the performance of the system around it.

Process stability is a necessary condition for continuous improvement. This kind of thinking is where you begin to cross the line from software development into software engineering.

ACCOUNTING FOR BUGS AND REWORK

How do you handle bugs and rework in a software development kanban system?

One way or another, buggy work-in-process is still in process and counts against the total WIP limit. The only question is which part of the workflow gets stuck with a kanban token for rework.

BUG SCENARIO

Here we have a two-stage work package decomposition. Green tickets represent a "requirement" work item. These could be something like Use Cases, or they could be Functional Requirements, etc. What matters is that they are something that represents customer value and seem like a "thing" to analysts, UI designers, testers, and the like.

These are decomposed into smaller work items for developers. Each yellow ticket represents a "feature," in the spirit of Feature-Driven Development (FDD). Each feature will be designed, reviewed, coded, tested, reviewed, and integrated into a development branch. When all of a requirement's features are complete, they will be rolled back up for review between analysis, testing, and development, merged into the test branch, and approved for functional verification and validation.

We should expect that bugs will be found from time to time, though we hope that this happens with decreasing frequency as a team matures. In this example, we have two requirements in testing, and they have found three bugs so far (blue tickets).

The question is: what do we do with these bugs, now that we have found them? Let's consider two options: 1) Reinsert defective WIP into an upstream station, 2) Assign bugs to a shared rework station. Each case has pros and cons, which depend on circumstances, like process maturity.

OPTION 1: REINSERT DEFECTIVE WIP UPSTREAM

In this scenario, we've taken the kanban for work item R5 out of the Test station and placed it back in Development, where it is treated like any other requirement work item. When it is complete, it will be placed back in the Resolved:Ready queue and retested. It will be subject to all of the usual limits and rules along the way. The kanban is charged to Development, and Test is free to pick up the next thing that appears in their Ready queue.

This is the softer approach. It is less disruptive and it treats bugs with less urgency. A downside of treating rework like a regular work item is that if Development capacity is full, then the buggy work item will have to be placed in a queue to wait its turn.

The attitude here is that bugs are an expected common cause variation.

OPTION 2: SHARED REWORK STATION

In this scenario, we're leaving the kanban for work items R4 and R5 in test and moving the bug kanban to a special rework station. Test may continue to work on R4 and R5 while the rework is done, but since they are at capacity, they can't pull in any new work. That means that the bugs have to be treated like an expedited request. Otherwise, the system will stall until they are resolved.

This is the harder approach. It treats the bugs like a process failure that must be attended to immediately. The kanban is still allocated to the Test station, and the Rework station does not count against the Development limit. Since the rework station is dedicated, there's no waiting for a slot to open up in development. Regardless, development capacity will be reduced because people will have to give priority to the bugs in order to make space to resolve the regularly scheduled work items.

The attitude here is that bugs are a special cause variation and call for corrective action. This might be the right configuration if a team or project is new, or the team is having an acute quality problem. Once they get the problem under control, they can relax to the reinsertion model.

POOL QUEUE

Manufacturing systems have workflows and knowledge work systems have workflows (and little lambs eat ivy). There are principles that apply to workflows in general, regardless of whether they operate on bits or atoms. There are also things that are completely different about information workflows. One of those things is the physical space necessary to operate the system. The nature of information space is fundamentally different from any physical process.

Fortunately for us, that often works to our advantage. It means we can manipulate our workflows and work products in ways that would be nonsensical to a traditional industrial engineer. Since most of the literature about Lean is still about moving atoms around, you have to pinch yourself every now and then as a reminder that moving bits around involves a different set of rules.

Bits or atoms, the notion of an inter-process inventory buffer is generally important to our scheduling methodology. Our overall goal is to minimize lead times for new work requests, and a great part of how we do that is by managing our in-process inventory very carefully. But an information inventory is different from a manufacturing inventory, in that it doesn't occupy exclusive space in a meaningful way. Our information WIP might go into a virtual queue, effectively infinite in size, with no definite order for queuing or dequeueing, and no conflict between objects in the queue. A virtual queue can be random-in-random-out in a way that's improbable for more spatially-oriented storage.

An issue that seems to come up regularly for development teams is how to distribute multiple work product types across the team's resources. One approach says dedicate resources to each product type, say, a couple of "feature teams" and some bug fixers, or a "front end" team and a "back end" team. Another approach says make a prioritization rule and assign all of the work to the common team. A kanban system enables us to use a hybrid approach that dedicates *capacity* to each work product type, without actually dedicating *people*.

Suppose we have a fairly simple, generic, 2-stage development process, common to all work product types:

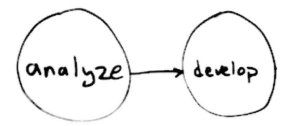

Because it's knowledge work, there's too much variation between the two subprocesses to synchronize according to a clock interval, so we make an inter-process queue to absorb the variation:

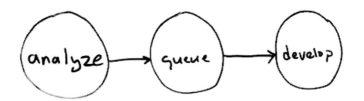

The queue just holds the kanban, the actual inventory is still sitting in the same document, database, or code repository that it was in when somebody was working on it. It doesn't matter where the real inventory is because nobody is competing for the storage.

Then we scale that process according to the available resources and demand:

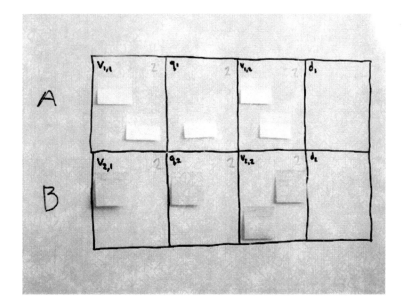

But we can hybridize even further by exploiting some of our "virtual space" advantage. Because our "workcells" and "buffer stocks" don't actually occupy any spatially constrained floor space, we can arrange them in any logical arrangement that suits us.

In this case, we're going to make a single pooled buffer that straddles both production lines:

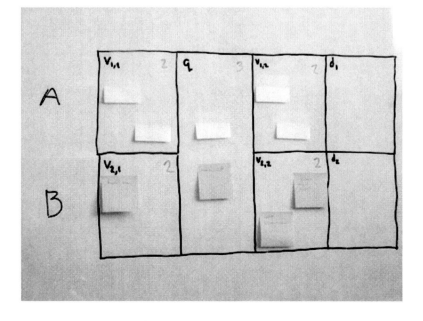

Why would we do that? Pooling the variation across the queues for both lines allows us to reduce the total number of kanban in the system, and thereby reduce the lead time for the system as a whole. The dedicated queues each needed a minimum capacity of 2, for a total of 4, to avoid stalling. The combined queue only needs 3 to avoid stalling, because it is rare that both independent queues are simultaneously at their limit of 2. We can reduce the queue further by improving the variability of either of the surrounding processes. Again, it will be easier to reduce from 3 to 2 than it would be to reduce from 2 to 1.

QUEUE UTILIZATION IS A LEADING INDICATOR

I've been getting into a lot of detail about how to apply Lean ideas to software development. Perhaps I sometimes take it for granted that we understand *why* we should apply them. Mary Poppendieck has already written quite a bit on that rationale, and I try not to rehash things I think she's already covered adequately. I do think there are a few characteristic scenarios where Lean principles most clearly apply to software development:

- Any kind of live network service, whether customer-facing (Google.com, Amazon.com) or machine-facing (Bigtable, SimpleDB)
- Any kind of sustaining engineering process: bug fixing, security patching, incremental enhancement
- Evolutionary product design (which is to say, effective product design)

That said, there is a very pragmatic reason to adopt a Lean workflow strategy, regardless of what sort of product you are building: *Lean scheduling provides crystal clear leading indicators of process health.*

I am speaking of kanban limits and andon lights.

WORK IN PROCESS IS A LEADING INDICATOR

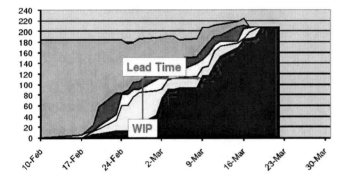

For a stable workflow, lead time is a function of both throughput (how much stuff we complete every day) and work-in-process. For a given rate of throughput (with everybody busy at his/her job), an increase in WIP necessarily means an increase in lead time.

This is simple cause and effect: an increase in WIP today will mean an increase in the time to deliver that work in the future. As far as leading indicators go, this one's rock solid. You can't do more work than you have the capacity to do work, without taking longer to do it.

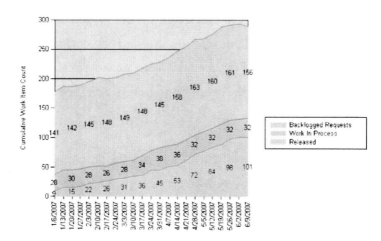

A simple management technique is to simplify the problem with policy. If lead time is a function of both throughput and WIP, and you can hold WIP near constant by an act of policy, then you can begin to address the more difficult problem of throughput. WIP is relatively easy to control, because somebody in your business should have the power to approve or deny starting on a new work order. Throttling work orders is a much easier problem than learning how to work faster.

This is effectively the result of a Drum-Buffer-Rope system, or its Lean cousin, a kanban system. Only after you get the simpler variable under control can you begin to make consistent progress on the more difficult one.

If we have a well-defined workflow, then the total work-in-process is the sum of the WIP of all of the parts of that workflow. Limiting the total WIP in the system can still mean quite a bit of variation in the distribution of

WIP between the parts of the system. Our next step after limiting total WIP will be managing that component WIP more closely, and it turns out that some parts of that component WIP are more sensitive predictors of lead time than others.

In other words,given the same root cause, some inter-process workflow queue will go from 2 to 4 long before the global WIP would go from 20 to 40 if left unregulated. If you set your system up correctly, one or more of those internal queues will telegraph problems well before they manifest elsewhere.

DEVELOPMENT WORKFLOWS NEED BUFFERS

The irregularity of requirements and the creative, knowledge-intensive nature of a design activity like software development rules out clocked workflow synchronization. Sometimes the interface to something will be simple, but the algorithm behind it will not. Sometimes the opposite is true. Sometimes an apparently simple design change has wide-reaching effects that require reverification and a lot of thinking about edge cases. Risk and uncertainty are built into the nature of development work. Novelty is what gives software its value, so you can only get so far in reducing this kind of variation before you have to mitigate and adapt to it.

Abandoning takt time for development work has been our big concession to the messy reality, although we still look for opportunities to introduce a regular cadence at a higher scale of integration. Of course, we'd be delighted and astounded to hear of anybody making a takt time concept work.

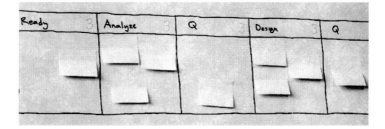

Instead, we have to use small inventory buffers between value-adding processes in order to absorb variation in the duration of each activity across work items. We allocate kanban to those buffers just like anywhere else, and those kanban count towards our total allocation. Making the buffers random-access makes them even more flexible in absorbing process variation.

What is this inventory? Specifications that have not been implemented. Designs that have not been reviewed. Code that has not been tested and deployed. You can measure things like "weeks of specs-on-hand" and "percentage of specs complete." The higher that first number is, the lower the second one probably is. For orgs that carry months' worth of specs at a time, that second number can quickly converge to zero. So don't do that! If you're carrying more than a few weeks worth of detailed specifications at a time, ask yourself….why? What are you going to do with them? Specification inventory is a liability just like any other kind of inventory.

So we're carrying a few hours or days worth of inventory at a time, because it's still faster than the alternatives of generalist labor or pipeline congestion. To be clear, when I'm talking about carrying kanban inventory, I'm talking about hours or days, not weeks or months. And I like hours a whole lot better than days.

THE JOY OF COMPLEMENTARY SIDE EFFECTS

Agile development has long rallied around the "inspect and adapt" paradigm of process improvement. It is a philosophy that it shares with its Lean cousin. But early Agile methods built their model of feedback around the notion of *velocity*, and velocity is a trailing indicator. Velocity, and even lead time, can only tell you about things that have already happened.

To be fair, all Agile methods include higher-frequency feedback in the form of the daily standup. But a qualitative assessment is not the same as a quantitative indicator. Done well, the right measure can tell you things that people in a conversational meeting either can't see or won't admit to. An informal, qualitative, Scrum style of issue management leads to confusion between circumstantial vs. systemic problems, and the obstacle-clearing function of the Scrum Master often leads to one of Deming's "two mistakes." But then, Deming might have taken exception to a number of beliefs and practices common to today's Agile practitioner. That's okay, we Planned and we Did, and now we are Studying and Acting.

The regulating power of the in-process inventory limit is it tells you about problems in your process *while you are experiencing the problem*. You don't have to extract a belated confession from a stubborn problem-solver or wait for the end of the month to have a review in order to notice that something went wrong. You watch it going wrong in front of your eyes as it happens.

In a kanban workflow system, inter-process queues start backing up immediately following any blockage in their downstream processes. If your team all works within a line of sight of a visual control representation of that inventory, then you see the problem together as it manifests. A backed-up queue is not a matter of opinion and the consequences are highly predictable.

MAKING THE INDICATOR WORK FOR US

If we're using a kanban system, we have the WIP limit indicator at our disposal. How can we use this to our advantage?

Under normal conditions of smooth flow, the kanban queues should be operating below their limits. Which is to say, the system has some slack. Slack is good, and optimum flow means "just enough slack." The limits for the queues are set according to a different rule than the limits for value-added states.

Buffer states are non-value-added processing time, so we want to make them as small as we can. The queues are there for the purpose of smooth flow. Make them too big, and they just increase inventory and lead time. Make them too small and they cause traffic jams...which also increases lead time. So there's a "just right" size for kanban queues, and that is *as small as possible without stalling X% of the time.*

Since the queue size is a tradeoff, there is an optimal value for X which is less than 100. The difference between X and 100 is your expectation of process improvement which will be triggered by the occasional stall event. So our process has slack, but our slack doesn't. When we run out of slack, we want to stop what we're doing and try to learn how to operate with less slack in the future.

A healthy state of affairs. A lot of working, not much waiting. When the next analysis task is done, there will be room to store the result, even if design is busy. Design is not under any particular pressure to complete something...yet. But conditions can change quickly, so no excuse to dawdle!

Since our system is a pull system, our process breaks down in a characteristic way. When a queue fills up, there's nowhere for the output of the process before it to go, so that process will begin to back up itself, and so on, until the entire pipeline in front of the jam eventually stops while the remainder of the pipeline flushes itself out.

Good! That's what we want. Every process in the system serves as a throttle for its predecessor. That means that the system as a whole is regulated by the health of its parts. Shortly after any part of the system starts to go wrong, the entire system responds by slowing down and freeing up resources to fix the problem. That automatic reflection of process health is a powerful mechanism for continuous improvement.

Let's walk through a typical failure mode:

1. Something is going wrong in the design process, but nobody knows it yet. The senior devs are all sick with the flu. Nobody signals the andon light because they're at home, or they have other problems on their minds.

2. The analysts, who are in a different hallway, seem immune and continue to complete their assignments. At this point, the process is already signaling that something is amiss.

3. The analysts start up their next tasks anyway. The pipeline to the right of design continues on processing from its own queue.

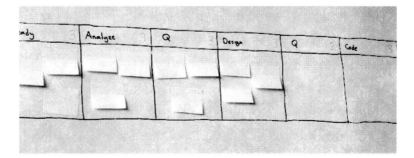

4. There's nowhere for the analysts to put their completed work, so now they are also stalled. The right side of the pipeline has flushed out whatever work was already in process and now they are idle as well. The ready queue has backed up, and so the whole pipeline is now stalled.

With no intervention other than enforcing the kanban allocation, the system spontaneously responds to problems by shutting itself down. This would be an example of jidoka applied to our development workflow. The people who are idled by this process can and should spend their time looking into the root cause of the problem, either to mitigate it (if it is a special cause) or to prevent it from happening in the future (if it is a common cause).

You can't really predict when the design team will get sick, so in this case, perhaps the analysts and junior devs can work together and complete some of the design tasks until the missing devs get back to health. In this case, it may be an opportunity to discover if the team is sufficiently cross-trained to cover the gap and ask questions about roles and responsibilities.

Even though the problem is self-limiting by slide 4, we already know in slide 2 that slides 3 and 4 are likely to happen if we don't intervene. It would have been better if somebody had taken greater notice of the signal in slide 2 and began an investigation. It would also be nice if the system itself could respond both more quickly and more gracefully than in this example.

Now we will look at another queuing method that will allow us to simultaneously reduce lead times, smooth out flow, and respond more quickly and gracefully to disruptions.

COMPLETION QUEUE AS INCREMENTAL THROTTLE

We've discovered some useful properties of internal workflow queues:

- Queue states between processes can provide an early warning of process breakdowns.

- Local work-in-process limits serve to slow down a malfunctioning workflow and free up resources to fix it.

- Queues can sometimes be combined to reduce the total work-in-process while still preserving their buffering function.

I gave an example of workflow throttling, and suggested another configuration of those internal queues that could respond more smoothly and gracefully than the simple, independent queues given in the example.

In order to pull a work item, there has to be a place to pull it from, and there should be some way to distinguish work that is eligible to be pulled from work that is still in process. At the same time, there has to be a place to put completed work when you are done with it. A completion queue serves both these functions.

In this case, we can have up to 3 items in the "specify" state AND we can have up to 3 items waiting for the next state in the workflow. The team can pull new work into "specify" whenever there are fewer than 3 work items in process. If there are already 3 work items in process then the team will have to wait until something is moved into the completion queue. If there is some kind of blockage downstream, first the completion queue will fill up, THEN the specify queue will fill up, THEN the specify process will stall. And when it stalls, it stalls all at once. The flow is either on or off, there's no middle speed, and it keeps going until it stalls.

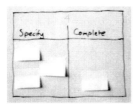

In another example, we still have a busy state and a complete state, but the token limit is shared between them. In this case, we can have 4 items in process OR 4 waiting. Or we can have (3 busy + 1 waiting) OR (1 busy + 3 waiting).

In the ideal case of 3 busy and 1 waiting, this queue works just like the first example does. However, if work starts to accumulate in the "complete" state, then the "specify" state will incrementally throttle down. The effective WIP limit for "specify" goes from 4->3->2->1->0 as more items are completed ahead of the rate of downstream intake. So, the process slows before it stops, and it slows much sooner than it would have under the independent queues.

What's more, even though it operates in the same way in the normal case, it does so with two fewer kanban in the system. Fewer kanban, with gradual throttling and smoother flow, should result in lower lead times.

With this in mind, let's reconsider our workflow stall scenario:

Ready	Specify	Complete	Design	Complete	Code	Complete

1. Something is going wrong in the design process, but nobody knows it yet.

2. The specify-complete queue starts to back up, thereby throttling down the WIP limit for specify. A resource is freed as a result, who should now inquire into the cause of the backup, which may only be random variation. The code process continues to complete work and pull from the existing backlog.

3. Code state begins to starve and specify state throttles down another level. Two more people are released as a result. There are more than enough free resources now to either fix the problem or shut down the process.

4. The stall completes by flushing out the specify and code states.

It still takes a while for the system to stall completely. The difference is that it *begins* stalling immediately, and when it does stall, it stalls with less WIP. For equivalent throughput, this pipeline should operate with fewer kanban and less variation in WIP, and therefore should have smoother flow and shorter lead times. It should respond faster to problems and free up resources earlier to correct those problems.

These shared completion queues might be the most common type of workflow queue. There are a few other types that we use, which are more advanced topics.

BETWEEN KANBAN AND PAIR PROGRAMMING LIES THE FEATURE BRIGADE

It is easy to understand why the Agile community rebelled against some of the traditional roles and responsibilities in software development organizations. Since the phase/gate model of project management aligns itself according to such roles, and Agile thought rightly identifies phase/gate as the primary disease afflicting the profession, it is predictable that anything associated with that model would also be considered suspect. Skepticism about division of labor also promotes an affinity with some with a "revolutionary" disposition, and I don't think it is controversial to suggest that Agile still holds considerable appeal for the rebellious.

The central management problem of product development remains:

> How do you coordinate communication between a large number of highly trained individuals working on a common problem that no one individual can fully comprehend?

The better part of any development process or
philosophy addresses just this issue.

Scrum and XP, like most processes, define a set of roles
for project participants. Some of those roles preserve or
reinforce conventional divisions of labor (product owner,
pigs/chickens), other roles seek to break down such
divisions (technology specialists, testers). To some
degree, the product owner role is a black box
placeholder for further roles that are not visible to the
core development team. One classic division
(requirements analysis) is strongly reinforced, both
through the product owner role, and by the transactional
barrier of iteration planning and product backlog.

Other divisions are broken down with new practices like
test-driven development and pair programming. TDD
automates the discovery of errors, so therefore has a
pretty clear Lean interpretation as an example of Jidoka
(of course, I still think Design by Contract is a better
example).

Pair programming is a bit more problematic with respect
to Lean, which is greatly concerned with the
conservation of labor. Slack capacity in a lean system
takes the form of facilities and equipment, and labor
capacity is highly optimized.

*"To improve operations, the Toyota production
system focuses on manpower cost reductions. By*

comparison, relatively little emphasis is placed on raising the operating rates, even though they are, along with man, the primary agents of production. The reason for this is straightforward: For a given period of time, the loss will be about five times greater for idle workers than for idle machines. Moreover, Toyota realized that no matter how low equipment operating rates might be, for the purposes of cost reduction, it was more effective to concentrate on human labor costs. Failure to grasp this point clearly and keep in in mind may well lead to a misunderstanding of the exact role that manpower cost reduction plays in the Toyota production system." — Shigeo Shingo, A Study of the Toyota Production System

To be sure, the relative proportion of value added by machines vs. people is going to be pretty different for knowledge work vs. manufacturing. At the least, you can interpret Shingo's advice as meaning it is stupid to cut corners on office space, computer monitors, and software tools–a mistake I see much more often than I would like. But it also means that the kind of labor redundancy of the practice of pair programming is pretty contrary to Lean.

I should point out that I'm only trying to distinguish "lean" vs. "not lean" here, rather than good vs. bad. Arguing what lean is good for is another discussion. If I haven't been clear about this before, I have been a great believer in "situational pairing" since about 1995. There are times when the uncertainty or complexity of a problem is sufficiently high that the cost of delay or failure clearly exceeds the cost of redundancy. I also believe that those times are not "all the time" or even "most of the time," but there are occasions when it is useful.

Kanban systems are a nearly orthogonal solution to the same problem of coordinating work and workers. Both kanban and pairing address the problem of workflow efficiency and loss due to handoffs. Kanban systems seek to exploit labor specialization advantage and optimize transaction efficiency. Pair development seeks to improve individual productivity and prevent errors and rework. Each approach depends on a tradeoff. Does productivity advantage exceed transaction overhead? Is a pair more productive than the sum of the individuals?

Kanban and pairing are not exclusive. The states in a workflow are best understood as processes and not people. Work moves from one process to the next *and then* people apply themselves to the process. Those people can be pairs of people as well as individuals. They could be a pair of similar skills, like conventional pair programming, or they could be a pair of mixed skills: analyst&programmer, programmer&tester, analyst&tester, etc. An analyst might decide to flow with the kanban to the next state if she feels that there is some uncertainty to the task that requires closer collaboration in design. I would expect a mature team to think in exactly this way. A great thing about pull systems for knowledge work is that they give people so much power over how they want to organize for particular tasks. Situational pairing is a pretty good way to offset some of the risk of handoffs. It is also something that lends itself to kaizen optimization.

A STEP TOWARDS ZERO BUFFER INVENTORY

There may be a third method that combines some of the strengths of kanban and pairing and reduces their respective weaknesses. A *bucket brigade* is a stockless self-leveling workflow with a dynamic division of labor.

A simple type of bucket brigade retrieves water from one source, like a river, and delivers it somewhere else, where it is needed. Each link in the brigade carries water from the direction of the source toward the destination until he meets another link traveling in the opposite direction. Then they exchange the bucket full of water for an empty bucket and the first link turns around and travels back toward the source.

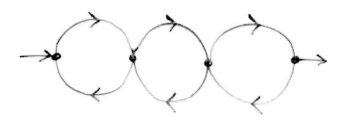

If this link is the middle of the chain, he will then meet another link carrying water from upstream and once again exchange the empty bucket for a bucket full of water, and turn around to meet the downstream link. When the receiver has gathered enough water, he can retire each carrier as they appear and take their buckets out of circulation. The last carrier will then travel the entire distance of the brigade and then retire.

Since the links in the brigade are likely people of different strength, speed, and endurance, covering different terrain, there will be differences in the amount of ground that each link covers in his circuit. Not only will there be different local capacities, but those capacities may vary considerably over time as each link takes short breaks, stumbles, or slowly wears down due to fatigue.

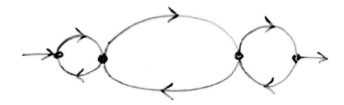

What's most interesting about the bucket brigade is that it is almost entirely self-regulating. No inventory buffers are needed to absorb variation in station cycle times. No conscious adjustments are required from the carriers in order to adapt. Handoffs are directly triggered by downstream availability. Capacity can easily be added or subtracted by adding or removing links from the chain and the system will spontaneously redistribute the work load in response.

The value added by the process is the transportation of the water. The water has value and the labor expended to move it downstream adds value. The labor required to move the buckets back upstream, however, does not add value. It is waste, but perhaps necessary waste. What can we do to reduce this waste?

You could think of this simple bucket brigade as utilizing only 50% of available capacity. We could utilize the other 50% by sending something back upstream. Perhaps we could send greywater back up to be dumped in the river (assume that the upstream users have a stake in the local ecology, and that the greywater does not contaminate the river).

Generalizing this makes the bucket the kanban–an order for more work. There only need to be as many buckets as there are carriers to handle them, and they only stay in circulation as long as there is demand. If there were multiple sources, the bucket-kanban could be marked with instructions about what to put in the bucket by the final picker.

Just as kanban systems can be generalized from supply chains or assembly lines, a bucket brigade can be generalized for arbitrary workflow management. "Bucket brigade" may not sound sufficiently dignified for the matter at hand, so perhaps for our purposes we can call it a *feature brigade*.

THE OPERATION OF A FEATURE BRIGADE

A kanban system is a more flexible division of labor than any phase/gate system, while still being stable and well regulated. Role definitions can be adjusted by kaizen updates to workflow or procedures. Work orders can be pulled by any available cross-trained team member, and workers can flow downstream to collaborate with the next station. Nonetheless, work transitions still occur only at well defined points, and inventory buffers are necessary to synchronize tasks of variable duration so that downstream workers do not have to wait for new work orders. Inventory can be costly, but idle workers are more so.

A feature brigade has most of the advantages of a discrete workflow, but can be (and must be) even more flexible. Any two adjacent workers must have overlapping skills, because where and when they meet is not predetermined.

A simple case would be a 3-person one-way feature brigade, with an analyst-designer, a designer-coder, and a coder-tester. Any time the coder-tester considers himself to be finished with his current feature, he checks it in as complete and signals the designer-coder. Since the coder-tester is also a coder, he interrupts the designer-coder at any time during coding and takes responsibility for her current feature. If the designer-coder thinks she is at a good transition point, then she may just hand over what she has, with a specification and a walkthrough. It is more likely that they will collaborate for a while on the same feature until she believes that the coder-tester understands it well enough to continue independently. In other words, they will pair program. Once she hands off, then in turn, the designer-coder will signal the analyst-designer that she is ready to start working on the next feature, resulting in a pair design session.

That's a pretty interesting scenario, but we've introduced a coordination problem between the analyst-designer and the coder-tester. How does the coder-tester know the intent of the analyst-designer? Why would the analyst-designer trust the judgment of the coder-tester to validate the results? In order to make this work, a lot more detail will have to go into the specification in order to convey the intent of the analyst. Most of that additional work is non-value-added process overhead.

It would be better to find a way to include the analyst more directly in validation. Fortunately, this isn't the first time this question has come up in software engineering methodology. The V-Model of software development was invented to address the same problem in the Waterfall Model. While we still aim to implement a pull system, perhaps we can learn from what the V-Model did to address this flaw.

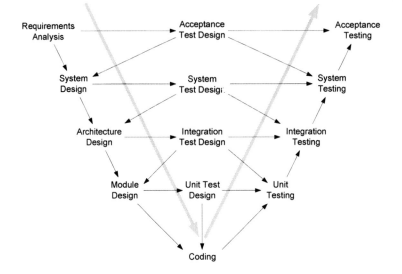

The V Model attempts to improve quality and reduce rework by explicitly pairing each value-adding step of the development workflow with a verification or validation step. It requires some kind of coordination activity between the "downstream" operator and the corresponding "upstream" operator before the work can be promoted to the next step in the workflow.

One could argue (and I do) that the Extreme Programming workflow is a modern interpretation of the V Model, where one-piece flow has replaced the old phase/gate packaging of work requests. A similar interpretation applies to the SEI Personal Software Process, which itself can be modified to be more feature-oriented.

At this point, we can see if the symmetry of the V Model and the symmetry of our bi-directional bucket brigade can be combined to address the coordination problem of our first feature brigade.

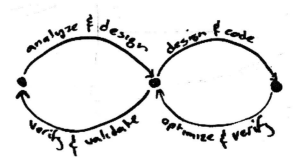

A simple two-person feature brigade has each link alternating between development and verification activities. Each person verifies the work coming upstream that they had previously passed downstream. At each handoff, there is an opportunity to collaborate with an adjacent link on both the downstream and the upstream exchanges.

To visualize, this system would operate in alternating phases. In the odd phase, the analyst-designer is (oddly enough) analyzing and designing, and the designer-coder is optimizing and verifying. In the even phase, the designer-coder is designing and coding, while the analyst-designer is verifying and validating. Because the analyst-designer and the designer-coder are both designers, it doesn't much matter when they meet for the handoff. The more skilled the analyst-designer is, the more work he will complete before the hand off.

In this way, the system is self-leveling. The more the skill of the designer-coder improves, the earlier he will be able take possession of the kanban. Furthermore, the handoff does not have to be a simple exchange. In fact, this is where the synthesis of kanban and pair programming occurs. The handoff can be an extended collaboration, where the analyst-**designer** and the **designer**-coder work together on **design**, until they agree that they both have a common understanding of the problem and the designer-coder can successfully complete the design on his own.

This makes the feature cycle a little bit more elaborate, but not by much. There is now an alternation between working together and working independently.

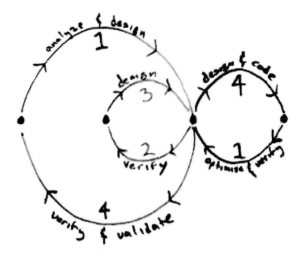

In the first phase, the analyst-designer is analyzing and designing the ith feature and the designer-coder is optimizing and verifying the i-1th feature.

In the second phase, the analyst-designer and the designer-coder are both verifying the i-1th feature, as a pair.

In the third phase, the analyst-designer and the designer-coder are both designing the ith feature, as a pair.

In the fourth phase, the analyst-designer is verifying and validating the i-1th feature, and the designer-coder is designing and coding the ith feature.

Then the whole cycle starts again with the i+1th feature.

The cost of introducing this bidirectional model is a small swap buffer during the collaborative phase. Since each worker is holding one kanban, and they can only work on one at time while they are collaborating, then the other kanban must be idle for some part of the handoff period:

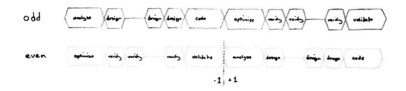

You can see that the "swap buffer" idle period is fairly small relative to the rest of the value stream. That gap is the productivity advantage we have to realize from specialization in order to benefit from the feature brigade strategy.

Since we've introduced this notion of an extended collaborative handoff, we can interpret pure pair programming as a special case. We can also interpret a fixed-transition kanban system as a special case of an instant handoff. Finding such a hybrid enables us to apply the benefits of either extreme, or offset the disadvantages of either extreme. We can realize some of the benefits of pairing, like cross-training and continuous peer review, with some of the benefits of kanban, like pull and specialization advantage.

We started with a simple division by job function, but there are other collaborative relationships we can manage by this method. A complex feature may involve collaboration across technical specialties, like user interfaces and database. We can also use the self-leveling mechanism to introduce new people in a project in a way that minimizes their disruption and accelerates their learning.

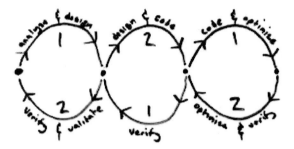

Like any bucket brigade, the bidirectional feature brigade scales out to three or more links. You can continue to pair at each meeting as well. Three or more links forms a 6-phase cycle, where the pairs alternate in an even+odd, odd+even sequence. It makes a lovely graph, but I'll leave you to draw that as an exercise!

You might begin to worry about synchronizing a 6-phase cycle, but don't! The feature brigade is entirely self-synchronizing. People meet when they meet, and overlapping skills and pairing absorb all of the variation.

PRIORITIZING AND PLANNING

RELEASE EARLY, RELEASE OFTEN

The first time I heard that particular phrase was probably Jim McCarthy's *Dynamics of Software Development* in the mid-1990's. Not only is it still the right guidance, but now we can more provide more mature reasoning about what that means and why it's the right goal.

DETERMINE THE MINIMUM DEPLOYABLE FEATURE SET, AND THEN BUILD THAT AS FAST AS YOU CAN

If you are in the car building business and the design of your transmission isn't done yet, then you are simply not ready for production. On the other hand, if you are waiting on the dashboard navigation system or the retractable cup holders, then the opportunity cost of delay probably outweighs any incremental value those requirements will deliver. Ship now, and when those features are ready, roll them into production.

If you ask Marketing what the minimum deployable feature set is, you aren't likely to get a very helpful answer. The minimum feature set has to be about logical completeness. A car without a transmission is illogical. A car without a motorized heated cup holder is not. When you can't take anything else away without making the system clearly nonsensical, then you've found the minimum set. Some of the matrix-based design techniques like Axiomatic Design can help you figure this out more formally.

For every feature that you add beyond the minimum deployable set, but without deployment, your costs now include all of the revenue that you are not generating from the product that you could have released, in addition to your ongoing operating expenses. If the goal of your business is to make money, then you want to start realizing those earnings sooner rather than later.

Even if a competitor has launched ahead of you with a larger feature set, don't try to compete with them on scope. Compete on productivity. If your business produces new features at a faster rate, it won't take you long to overtake them. If that faster rate is also steadily increasing (an expected outcome of a Lean process) at a faster rate, then you will quickly leave them in the dust. Know this and manage accordingly.

WHEN YOU'RE DESIGNING YOUR DESIGN PROCESS, FIRST VISUALIZE THE IDEAL FINAL RESULT

TRIZ is a treasure chest of useful ideas, and one I have found especially fruitful is the notion of the Ideal Final Result (IFR). IFR is the perfect action or outcome in the abstract. It is free of any mechanism, and any constraints of the solution domain, in a world without friction, without entropy, and without costs. If you can imagine your ideal state or your ideal function without any of this extraneous noise, then you can start to introduce real mechanisms in a way that facilitate that outcome with the least interference. At the very least, the IFR gives you something to be dissatisfied with in your inexhaustible quest for perfection.

In microprocessors, the Ideal Final Result might be an infinite number of infinitesimally small transistors with zero energy consumption. Moore's Law describes how real microprocessors evolve in the direction of this ideal.

In pull scheduling, One Piece Flow is the ideal result. A Value Stream identifies all of the processing steps that are applied to component materials in order to make the desired product. The word *stream* implies that there is a smooth, unbroken flow between a sequence of processing steps. Part of this can be achieved by allowing downstream states to pull work items from upstream states when capacity becomes available to do work. This can be implemented with a kanban system.

Another part of smooth, unbroken flow can be achieved by partitioning workflow states such that each is of a similar duration. Another part is defining work item requests so that they are of similar size and therefore require a similar duration to complete. Still another part is pulling quality assurance steps earlier into the process in order to reduce backflows between workflow states.

When these things have been done, it is possible for work requests to flow smoothly through the development process with a predictable lead time, cycle time, and resource utilization. A continuous smooth flow of valuable new features into deployment is the Ideal Final Result.

A FEATURE IS DEFINED AS THE MINIMUM TESTABLE UNIT OF CUSTOMER VALUE

What constitutes testing should ultimately derive from something that represents customer utility. Quality Function Deployment describes in exhaustive detail the kinds of transformations that yield specific tests from a model of customer needs.

By identifying a feature as both something small and as something a customer could identify as having specific value, we enable a scheduling discipline where work can always be quantified in financial terms. Furthermore, that work is mostly additive, where every time we complete a work item, we have a measurably more valuable asset. Document- and plan-heavy processes often dig cavernous pits of sunk costs before they begin to deliver a single nugget of customer utility. That is a very risky and ultimately quite irresponsible way to run a business.

MINIMIZING WORK-IN-PROCESS ALWAYS APPLIES, EVEN WHEN THE DEPLOYMENT SET IS LARGE

Deployment batch size is a function of two independent inputs: 1) the production capability of the supplier, and 2) the consumption capability or preference of the consumer. One of these is probably the limiting factor that governs the total batch size. Good customer service means that you'd prefer to let the customer determine that size rather imposing your own limitation upon them. This means you should develop the capability to deliver smaller, more frequent deployment packages than your customers are currently asking for. Once your customers realize that they can take more targeted and incremental updates, then they may start to choose that option, likely to their advantage over customers that do not.

But even if they don't, controlling your own internal inventory will yield large and increasing improvements to your own business efficiency. Lean production is probably the single greatest enabler of continuous improvement. Most development organizations struggle to achieve even linear productivity growth, but Lean development is *all about compound productivity growth.* Successful implementation of a Lean production line is likely to yield a dramatic boost in the first year, as capacity is balanced against demand, and the easily identified waste is driven out of the system. A 100%

first year productivity improvement would not be unexpected from a successful Lean launch.

PRIORITY FILTER

Planning and prioritizing is a wicked problem that has plagued humankind since time immemorial.

Suppose your next release has 100 features planned. If you ask your product manager to prioritize those features from 1 (high) - 3 (low), you're likely to get a response like:

```
80 x priority 1
15 x priority 2
 5 x priority 3
```

Maybe your product managers are more helpful than some of the ones I've worked with, but the above thinking sounds pretty familiar to me and reminds me of a formula:

If everything is high priority, then nothing is.

...which amounts to an abdication of responsibility for making a decision. There are several ways to approach that. The brute force method, which I like to call "Developer's Natural Authority," is:

If you refuse to take responsibility for sequencing the work, then I will.

That's a pretty aggressive position, but it helps to define a boundary of the problem. A somewhat more subtle approach is to repeat the question: "Of the 80 priority 1 features, please sort them into three equal-sized buckets." In response, your planning colleague might: a) cooperate with you, b) take the hint and do the right thing, or c) become irritated with your ploy and refuse to cooperate, in which case you are back to "DNA."

One of the problems here is that "high" or "priority 1" don't really mean anything unless you define them. As we've said here before (and will say again), plans and specifications are meaningless without operational definitions. So, we try to define what we mean by "priority 1."

Unfortunately, the usual approach to such a definition is a categorical description of priority levels: *a priority 1 feature has such-and-such value and so-and-so risk.* In practice, this rarely works well because it merely shifts the ambiguity out by one layer. Now we have to develop operational definitions of our otherwise subjective categories, and our little exercise is starting to look more and more complicated and expensive.

One way to respond to all of this is to apply some skills and get much more disciplined about prioritization. This is the path of methods like Quality Function Deployment or Analytic Hierarchy Process. I am a fan of these methods, so it is tempting to just stop there and insist on bringing more to the game. But that's not a very realistic or constructive attitude. Because while something like AHP might be appealing to a methodology geek like me, most of the people I work with are just looking for simple solutions to their immediate problems.

Effective prioritization will always define a relatively small number of high priority work items. The usual approach to this is to define some absolute criteria that separate out a few features from the rest, considered together. Then, the sequence of the work will simply be to complete all of the priority 1 features, followed by all of the priority 2 features, and then the priority 3 features, until time runs out.

But why be so absolute? The value added by prioritization is effective sequencing, and further information that is created in consequence is probably wasted effort. Rather than a monolithic absolute priority ranking, why not use something more incremental and relative? Why should we care what the 37th work item from now will be, when we only need to know what the next one is? I'm pretty sure the answer is that we don't care.

What we really want is a method that allows us to make good sequencing decisions as late as possible and for the lowest incremental cost. Which, of course, sounds like a call for pull and options thinking. The approach

I've been using lately is a kanban-like method I call "Progressive Priority Filter" or "Priority Sieve."

Here I have drawn a task planning board with five columns. The columns are labeled *backlog, pri 3, pri 2, pri 1,* and *done.* The three priority columns contain work item tickets, and each column has a work-in-process limit. The limit decreases by priority. We define priority according to situational capacity and availability, rather than by some absolute product criteria.

Our priority definitions are something like:

1. An item which we are currently working on or intend to work on immediately, strictly limited by our currently available capacity

2. An item which we should work on as soon as possible, but for which we do not have immediate capacity

3. An item which we should work on soon, but is not immediately pressing

The limit for priority 1 is strictly defined by current capacity, which is how much work can be done today, or a similarly convenient minimum planning interval. If you have a work capacity of 2, then there are always 2 priority 1 work items. Regardless of how much work has been done or how much work remains, at all times exactly 2 work items have priority 1 with respect to the existing backlog.

The limits for priorities 2 and 3 should be defined by some increasing sequence, such as geometric (e.g. 2,4,8) or Fibonacci (e.g. 3,5,8). Such a sequence should match the uncertainty of the decision. Pri 3 tickets are much less certain than pri 1 tickets, so we keep more of them open as "options." Such an increasing sequence also means that tickets spend more time in the lower priority states than the higher ones, befitting their uncertainty.

The priority buffers are followed by a larger backlog of items defined as *items which we believe we should do, but do not yet have priority*. If a new item appears in the backlog that is obviously more important than something on the board, then that new item may replace an item on the board, which is returned to the backlog. This can be done for any item that is not already in process. The backlog is only limited by space on the board, and backlog items are written directly on the board, without a ticket. A backlog item is only considered serious enough to merit a ticket when it is promoted to priority 3.

Naturally, any time a work item is complete, it is moved to the "done" column:

Completing a work item makes capacity available, and triggers a process for making a priority decision:

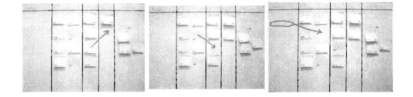

Only three items need to be selected per decision, and only one selection constitutes a commitment (pri2->pri1). Each item will be considered at least three times before being promoted from backlog to priority 1, and there is plenty of opportunity to demote it before it makes it that far. The cost of making each scheduling decision is low, and the probability of committing to a poor decision is also low. There is ample opportunity for the team to review and modify the current priorities, as the only negotiated tickets are the small number of priority 1's, which should only be selected with the consent of the task's owner.

One more element is needed to make this viable as a prioritization scheme. It might be possible for a ticket to languish in the lower priority states without ever being selected for promotion. To prevent this, new tickets should be given an expiration date. When tasks in one priority bucket are compared in consideration for promotion, aging tickets should be given preferential consideration. Old tickets deserve either immediate promotion or reconsideration, but should not be allowed to languish in a buffer indefinitely.

I like this system because it seems to strike a good balance between overhead and outcome. Like AHP, it breaks the problem into small chunks that are easily considered. Unlike AHP, it defers decisions until they are actually required, and when more information is available. Thus, it's also a bit like Rolling Wave Planning, in the small. Each decision is limited in scope, and only a portion of each decision makes a commitment. It minimizes the penalty of making suboptimal choices. It broadcasts the current state of understanding and delegates responsibility to the team with minimum overhead. These are all features that I want in a prioritizing process, so if there is a better scheme than this one, it will still have to meet this bar.

PERPETUAL MULTIVOTE FOR PULL SCHEDULING

If we're going to schedule one work item at a time, then we need a reliable method of picking the next item. Sometimes the work has a natural order and more-or-less picks itself. Other times, we have a backlog of things to choose from and have to make a decision. This is not so much a prioritization problem as it is a filtering problem. We don't care about the 30th priority feature in the backlog. We only care about the 1st priority feature. That should make it more a matter of eliminating things we're not going to do now, rather than sorting things that we may do someday.

The priority also has to be "always live." In our system, development capacity can free up at any time. When it does, the next candidate should have been previously selected so that the team can get right to work. That means we'll have to make frequent updates to the selection process. If we're going to do this frequently, it has to be inexpensive. Consensus building is expensive. My goal is to do this with no estimates and no meetings.

My first proposal was to create fixed-size priority buckets and make work items compete for space in those buckets until they rose to the top. I labeled this idea the "priority filter," and I've been using it for a few months. After some discussion about it, I asked for a Digg-like or prediction-market-like scheme. Eric Landes proposed some kind of multivoting system. Then Eric Willeke chimed in, and I started to focus on a new concept, which I'm calling *perpetual multivoting*. I've participated in a lot of multivotes, but I've never seen a continuous multivote.

votes	feature	date

I don't know if we reached a perfect consensus, but this is my current interpretation:

- A "voting committee" is selected, representing a fair cross-section of stakeholder interests - producers and consumers. Each voting member is assigned a color and an allocation of votes.

- The voting members can add an item to the selection backlog at any time. Backlog items are date stamped. When the list overflows, the oldest thing is ejected to make room.

- Voters may cast or recast their votes at any time, and they may cast multiple votes for a single item.

- When the pull event occurs, the top-voted item is immediately selected. In the event of a tie, a tie-breaker vote will be called. The votes from the selection are returned to a vote pool. Their owners are expected to recast them as soon as possible. If a pull event occurs and there are votes in the pool, the voters will be nagged.

EXPEDITING AND SILVER BULLETS

The pursuit of throughput will lead any production manager to try to smooth out flow through the process and regulate its input in order to minimize disruptions to smooth flow.

There are a variety of methods that can be applied to accommodate expected variation in work requests. But sometimes unexpected variation occurs and intervention is required to manage it with minimum disruption. If we knew everything that was going to happen, we'd just make a Gantt chart and be done with it. Most everybody here knows the world isn't like that, so we have to expect the unexpected and be prepared to deal with it.

Sometimes a critical work request comes along that the business did not plan for, but still requires immediate attention. For these cases, we have a special expedited request token that we call the "silver bullet."

A silver bullet is like a VIP pass that lets you cut to the beginning of the line. A silver bullet still has to go through the workflow. It is still subject to the WIP limits, and it is not allowed to interrupt work-in-process. If you were a VIP at a restaurant, you might get the first table to come up, but you don't get to kick anybody out who is already seated. At least, not at a respectable restaurant. For each state in the workflow, the silver bullet is automatically the first item to be selected for any available capacity.

There is only one silver bullet token, so only one can be in effect at any particular time. The engineering team asks the business to reserve expediting requests for truly exceptional circumstances. Everybody has seen the evidence that expedited requests disrupt flow and reduce productivity following the special event.

Work requests are normally selected and scheduled for development by a committee of business representatives who nominate requests for eligibility in one of the limited slots available. This same committee also has the authority to designate a work request as a silver bullet. Because the committee members represent different business functions, there is some competition to pick work proposals for the limited capacity. This creates an incentive to make a rational business case for your personal proposal. Most Vice Presidents don't like to see other Vice Presidents win shouting contests or get preferential treatment.

This competitive preference for fair selection also serves to discourage the use of the silver bullet. A silver bullet, by definition, will deprioritize work that is already in process, which was a high priority to a stakeholder in a previous round of work selection. A silver bullet allows one stakeholder to deprioritize the work requests of other stakeholders after the fact.

A silver bullet requires unanimous approval, and unanimous approval is hard to come by. Most have come to see this as a good thing.

ABOUT MODUS COOPERANDI

Corey Ladas has been an enthusiastic student of software engineering methodology since the early 1990's. Encouraged by the cross-disciplinary advancements of the Design Patterns movement and the eclectic approach of Steve McConnell's *Rapid Development*, Corey went off in search of unconventional inspiration from the worlds of systems engineering, industrial engineering, and product development. Lean Thinking is one of Corey's favorite discoveries from that process, and he has been experimenting with Lean methods in software development since the early 2000's. Corey's work in Lean development eventually brought him into collaboration with David Anderson, with whom he developed many of the practices and ideas contained in this book.

Modus Cooperandi is a private consultancy, located in the city of Seattle. Our focus is on organizational communication, which we approach from both the organizational design angle and the communication angle. We aim to provide thought leadership through books, blogs, and white papers. We provide training and consulting, and we develop software to support the management practices that we promote.

If you find the ideas and practices in this book to be relevant and compelling, Modus Cooperandi offers a condensed project launch consulting package. Our project launch package includes sufficient training and coaching to launch a small to medium-sized project team with a core lean development workflow, management practices, and performance metrics.

More information about Modus Cooperandi consulting services can be found at http://www.moduscooperandi.com

BIBLIOGRAPHY

The Machine that Changed the World, James Womack, Daniel Jones, and Daniel Roos, Simon & Schuster, 1990

Lean Thinking, James Womack and Daniel Jones, Free Press, 1996

Lean Solutions, James Womack and Daniel Jones, Free Press, 2005

The Goal, Eliyahu Goldratt, North River Press

Critical Chain, Eliyahu Goldratt, North River Press

A Study of the Toyota Production System, Shigeo Shingo, Productivity Press, 1989

Toyota Production System, Taiichi Ohno, Productivity Press, 1988

Rapid Development, Steve McConnell, Microsoft Press, 1996

A Discipline of Software Engineering, Watts Humphrey, Addison-Wesley, 1995

Introduction to the Team Software Process, Watts Humphrey, Addison-Wesley, 1999

Out of the Crisis, W. Edwards Deming, MIT CAES, 1982

Managing the Design Factory, Donald Reinertsen, Free Press, 1997

Extreme Programming Explained, Kent Beck, Addison-Wesley, 1999

Agile Software Development with Scrum, Ken Schwaber and Mike Beedle, Prentice Hall, 2001

Lean Software Development, Mary and Tom Poppendieck, Addison-Wesley, 2003

Lean Software Strategies, Peter Middleton and James Sutton, Productivity Press, 2005

Software by Numbers: Low-Risk, High-Return Development, Mark Denne and Jane Cleland-Huang, Prentice Hall, 2003

Agile Management for Software Engineering, David Anderson, Prentice Hall, 2004

First, Break All the Rules, Marcus Buckingham and Curt Coffman, Simon & Schuster, 1999

Managing the Development of Large Software Systems, Winston Royce, 1970

A Spiral Model of Software Development and Enhancement, Barry Boehm, 1988

Future of Scrum: Parallel Pipelining of Sprints in Complex Projects, Jeff Sutherland, 2005

CPSIA information can be obtained at www.ICGtesting.com
Printed in the USA
LVOW06s0625160814

399309LV00001B/64/P